Politics for People

Forrest David Mathews

POLITICS FOR PEOPLE

Finding a Responsible Public Voice

UNIVERSITY OF ILLINOIS PRESS
Urbana and Chicago

This book is printed on acid-free paper.

Library of Congress Cataloging-in-Publication Data

Mathews, Forrest David, 1935–
    Politics for people : finding a responsible public voice / David Mathews.
      p.   cm.
    Includes bibliographical references and index.
    ISBN 0-252-02088-X. — ISBN 0-252-06382-1 (pbk.)
    1. Political participation—United States. 2. Political culture—
United States. 3. United States—Politics and government—
1945–1989. Political leadership—United States—Public opinion.
5. Public opinion—United States. I. Title.
JK1764.M38   1994
323'.042'0973—dc20   93-5794
                                            CIP

Contents

Acknowledgments

To generations of research assistants, who may have wearied—
but never faltered,

To my secretaries, who cheerfully typed when fingers surely
rebelled,

To all who read and edited what must have seemed endless re-
visions,

To the citizens of the National Issues Forums, who brought
their toughest questions to the text,

To my colleagues in and around the Kettering Foundation,
who cooled many a hot August of writing with breezes of encouragement,

To all, I acknowledge a great debt of appreciation.

Introduction

Popular discontent erupted in American politics in the early 1990s with the force of a pent-up volcano. The upheaval was so dramatic that it obscured its own context—the erratic but ever-increasing popularization of politics in our republic. From President Jackson's unruly inaugural guests to angry populists in the next century to the champions of civil rights in our time, citizens demanding more attention, more access, and more power have marched their way onto the pages of our history, welcomed or not. Contemporary citizen discontent may actually be a prelude to still another rise in popular participation. So the question is not whether to put the public back into politics. Angry citizens have already made their presence felt. The question is what impact this latest wave of popular intervention will have.

The result may not be a stronger democracy. Greater popularization is not necessarily greater democratization. The consequences that follow from popularization are not preordained. They can be superficial and inconsequential, adding to people's frustrations and cynicism, if citizen participation is romanticized as it has been in the past. The effects of popularization can even be destructive, actually countering the good objectives of civic activism, or the effects can be constructive if more and more people come to politics as a responsible public.

A new wave of popularization, of greater access and more attention to popular opinion, will require much more of citizens. If people have more of a say, what they say will be more important. So this is a book about how "the people" might become a responsible public.

Of course, many Americans hate politics; they don't want to be put back into business as usual.[1] "Politics" makes them think about what they see on television and read in the newspaper: massive and indifferent bureaucracies, corrupt officials, pressure tactics, negative campaigns, and crowds screaming at one another. In other words, it is a mess. The elections of 1992 marked a suspension of this hostility but not an elimination of its causes. Many people will still tell you they aren't involved in politics and that politics has nothing to do with their lives.

Yet, these same people—the ones you see in factories and shops, that you pass at the malls and on the streets, the people who live around you—are deeply concerned about the common problems that confront everybody every day. They are concerned about having clean water to drink, having a good job and affordable health care, being safe from drugs and crime, and getting a good education for their children. These are what people call "the things that matter." And they are all political issues. In the 1992 elections, citizens took every opportunity to make the candidates stay focused on these substantive issues. They watched the debates in record numbers and, when given an opportunity to ask their own questions, they generally focused on the things that mattered. People wish that politics dealt more with these common problems. And although busy with other concerns, Americans will take time out for this kind of politics if they see any possibility of making a difference.

This book is about a politics that is more than what politicians do. It is about a politics that people actually practice—yet never call "politics."

Working together with others to solve common problems re-creates a sense of community that people like.[2] Americans deeply regret the loss of community. They believe that people should know their neighbors and help one another. They fear deep divisions in society and the conflicts among those of different races and beliefs. They find themselves confronted by a multitude of problems that grow out of a lack of community—and that further exacerbate the loss of community—problems that range from street crime to decreased competitiveness in a world economy.

The curious thing is, people don't think of working with others to solve common problems as "politics." They call what they do "community involvement" or "public activity." Americans seem to have lost that broader sense of politics that goes beyond what governments do. They have lost the names for what citizens do. The very idea of citizenship has eroded. Therefore, this book proposes a reconsideration of what politics is, who "owns" it, and who is responsible for it. It is a book about citizen or public politics—not about citizens as consumers or voters or taxpayers. It is about citizens as the primary officeholders in a democracy.

This book has two major sections. The first is on the way Americans react to politics as usual; the second (beginning with chapter 6) is on the way people feel about the politics they don't call politics—the politics of public problem solving and community involvement. Each begins with a report on what people actually say. These reports are followed by more interpretive chapters that try to account for why Americans act and react as they do. They also suggest what citizens might do to make politics more like what they want it to be. These suggestions grow out of what some people are already doing to make politics work for them.

Much of the information on how people feel about politics came from studies done by The Harwood Group, a public issues research and consulting firm in Bethesda, Maryland. Using focus groups, The Harwood Group did several studies of both citizens and officeholders. Some of this book is taken directly from these studies.[3] The quotations by people who are identified not by name but by location (Des Moines, Virginia, the West Coast) or occupation (a county commissioner) all come from the studies.

Focus group studies are quite different from polling. Representative groups of citizens have an opportunity to talk through issues and questions thoroughly. Such research doesn't claim to show what everybody thinks, yet it is a good indicator of perceptions and attitudes that are hard to gauge with other techniques.

Focus groups allow researchers to learn not only what people think about politics but also why they hold those views and how they think about them. This kind of information is often impossible to gather through opinion surveys. In surveys, questions need to be predefined for respondents to answer; people are unable to discuss issues and then reconsider their own views; and new information cannot be entered into a discussion for respondents to consider.

Still, the interpretations that emerge from focus groups need to be viewed as hypotheses that should be tested by other methods. The people who speak out in these groups can only testify to their personal experiences with politics. The validity of their conclusions ultimately rests on whether other people have had similar experiences and have come to similar conclusions.

One reaction to the Harwood study of citizens' views is that it grossly overstates the problem and is based on an idealized view of democratic possibilities. (Haven't Americans always been distrustful of government and cynical about political leaders?) Yet, as we read what people said, we can sense how deeply Americans feel about the problems of the political system and how justified they believe their expectations to be. Other studies may have reached similar conclusions, but what is powerful and compelling in the Harwood study are the voices of real people. They let us hear the tone and texture of what the public is saying. Their complaints are far too serious for electoral reforms or campaign finance laws to remedy. Although such reforms can be helpful, legal remedies by themselves aren't enough to address what people see as fundamental flaws in the political system.

This criticism fails to take into account what the public says about itself. The people quoted in this book are not just making excuses and looking for scapegoats. They believe that although decent folks go into politics, they are inevitably captured by a system so powerful that everyone must "play the game." People don't just blame politicians for the system. They know that the public itself is responsible. They know the public can also "play the game."

While the Harwood study found citizens angry about what they see happening in the political system, people are not unyielding cynics. Their anger comes from their idealism; America's sense of civic duty is not dead. Citizens are not indifferent to the issues that challenge our country. They look for things to do that have the possibility of bringing about change. Still, citizens have difficulty finding effective ways to act politically. Something seems missing in politics as usual; there seems to be little space for the public.

A sense of civic duty compels a number of Americans to work for fundamental change in the political system. Most of these people would also like to see reforms in government. They want government to be more effective at solving the problems that it is responsible for solving. But they want more; they want the political system to improve. This interest in better politics shouldn't be confused with interest in good government. They are different but related. Good government doesn't just mean efficient government, it means *our* government. This book is about how better politics can lead to better government.

Any book that makes a case for putting the public back into politics will trouble those who doubt the ability of ordinary people to be effective citizens, capable of making difficult decisions to advance the larger public interest. That includes those who genuinely wish that people were up to the demands of democratic citizenship. Before going on to the first chapter, a word needs to be said about these concerns.

First, putting the public back into politics does not mean that the public has to become the sole political actor, that direct democracy should replace representative government. Neither is popular opinion considered to be the voice of God. Obviously, people sometimes act in ways that are unworthy of citizens. Nonetheless, the citizens you will meet on these pages are more optimistic than pessimistic about their fellow citizens' ability to make sound decisions affecting their common life.[4] And the book is also optimistic about the public's ability to learn and to move from first impressions to more shared and reflective judgments about the interests of the public. But note that "the public" in this context refers to a deliberative body of citizens, not a mass of individuals. There is a great difference between what a direct or popular democracy can do and the abilities of a deliberative democracy.[5]

Still, under any circumstances there are doubts about people's competence to be effective citizens. The doubts usually take form in two charges. One is that the common people have neither the intellectual nor the moral capacity to make decisions about the well-being of society. And even if they did, the argument is that they wouldn't take the time. The other charge is that even if people have a measure of common sense and decency, the world in which they live is too complex for them to understand and too subject to centralized forces for citizens to control their own destiny. Those persuaded by these arguments look to elites to be guardians of the public's true interests and well-being. They cannot escape their pessimism, which they believe to be realistic or in accord with the "facts."

Optimism and pessimism, however, are attitudes or habitual ways of seeing the world; these worldviews are not the same as facts. There are not enough "facts" to convince the deeply pessimistic that ordinary people have the ability to govern themselves. There will always be cases of irresponsibility and selfishness to confirm their fears. Any evidence in this book to the contrary will never be persuasive to them.

Optimists, on the other hand, usually base their perspective on what they regard as common sense. Each individual has to have an equal stake in the decisions of the political community because those choices affect everyone's life. Therefore, people are political equals, with the right to make decisions about their shared fate. However unequal people may be in other respects, these inequalities are not thought to be so severe that only management by political elites can ensure a common well-being. This line of reasoning, long a characteristic of the optimist, is more fully laid out in Jeffrey Bell's *Populism and Elitism*.[6] Even some pessimists share this conviction. They urge citizens to take responsibility for the commonweal because they think it is necessary that people try to be the best citizens possible.

Those who rely on ordinary people are not naive. As Bell notes, they don't believe that "each voter has exactly the same ability as every other, or even that every group within the electorate is roughly equal to every other in level of education or political sophistication." They just believe in "the competence of the electorate to handle its own affairs relative to the competence of elites."[7] In the case of those citizens who are not as competent as others, optimists don't think their competence can be developed by consigning them to the guidance of more knowledgeable elites. They are confident in people's ability to learn, to grow as citizens by doing the work of citizens.

The distinction that Bell makes between those optimistic about citizens and those not has its limitations—as all generalizations do. Its value is to remind us that we are not just dealing with issues of fact but also with the influence of personal predilections and notions of what is fair. Still, even with these qualifications, the question remains, Is there any basis for optimism about citizens' abilities, other than a moral conviction about people's right to decide their own fate? Do people really know what they are talking about when they talk about the public's interest? Are people just too selfish and self-centered to act in the interest of their common well-being? And even if they try to act as citizens, is it just impossible—outside of some very local situations—for people to contend with a technology that overwhelms them and "the powers that be" that oppress them?

Americans who believe ordinary people must be—and can be—effective citizens have had some experiences that reinforce their optimism. Experiences are not the same as generalizable evidence. Experiences are what certain people have done in certain situations. No one argues that all of the people are good citizens all of the time. But if good citizenship can be found in some places some of the time, perhaps it can be found in more people, in more places, and on more occasions. Maybe politics doesn't always have to be as it is. Maybe we can do better. Some Americans believe in these possibilities even though they know full well that being a citizen isn't easy.

With each changing of the guard in the White House, we have a tendency to think that our problems will be solved. Deep in our hearts, however, we know better. For our democracy to work as we want it to, the public must do certain things. This book is about how the public can claim and act on its responsibilities. After all, if we criticize the political system because our role is too limited, it follows that many of the changes have to be citizen-initiated. Reforms from on high are hardly consistent with a quest for stronger democracy.

Notes

1. See Dionne, *Why Americans Hate Politics*.

2. The phrase *solving problems* is used often in this book because that is what people say they want politics to do—solve problems. However, there are no final solutions to political problems. No political solution is more than temporary, suitable only to some people for a limited time. Circumstances change, people change, and even the best solutions have unintended side effects that require a search for new solutions. Citizens understand this principle when they reflect on their civic work, as later sections of this book will show. People will often say that citizens acting responsibly is the only real solution.

3. See The Harwood Group, *Citizens and Politics* and Harwood, *The Public's Role in the Policy Process*.

4. In *Populism and Elitism* Bell uses the term *populism* to describe this belief. But because populism has so many other meanings, I have not used the term in this book.

5. For a clear description of the difference between deliberative and direct democracy, see Santiago Nino, *Deliberative Democracy and the Complexity of Constitutionalism*, ch. 5.

6. Bell, *Populism and Elitism*, 13.

7. Ibid., 11.

Part 1

Politics from the People's Perspective

We here highly resolve that these dead shall not have died in vain—that this nation, under God, shall have a new birth of freedom—and that government of the people, by the people, for the people, shall not perish from the earth.

—Abraham Lincoln

1

Forced Out of Politics by a Hostile Takeover

For many years, the conventional wisdom has said that the majority of Americans were apathetic about politics, that people just didn't care. Here is how one textbook described our political system to students: "If the survival of the American system depended upon an active, informed, and enlightened citizenry, then democracy in America would have disappeared long ago; for the masses of America are apathetic and ill-informed about politics and public policy, and they have a surprisingly weak commitment to democratic values. . . . fortunately for these values and for American democracy, the American masses do not lead, they follow."[1]

A study in 1991 of how people felt about politics—and why they felt as they did—provided some of the first evidence that Americans were not apathetic at all but were "mad as the devil" about a political system that has pushed them out of their rightful place in governing the nation. This was the Harwood study of *Citizens and Politics*, subtitled *A View from Main Street America*.

The Harwood study went beneath the usual popular dissatisfaction with government and politicians to discover strong feelings about powerlessness and exclusion, coupled with deep political concerns and an untapped sense of civic duty. According to the study, no interpretation of the public is less accurate than the often-repeated contention that people are apathetic and too consumed with private matters to care about politics. Certainly the people who participated in the study were far from apathetic. In fact, they were just the opposite; they had a clear sense of their civic responsibilities. They cared so deeply that their frustration ran to anger and cynicism—a cynicism they worried about passing on to their children. These Americans felt they had been pushed out of the political system by a professional political class of powerful lobbyists, incumbent politicians, campaign managers—and a media elite. They saw the system as one in which votes no longer made any difference because money ruled. They saw a system with its doors closed to the average citizen.

Symptoms of this public anger were evident for some time, but we didn't take them seriously. Low voter turnouts were so commonplace that they were almost expected. We tried to rationalize away the absence of this simplest form of participation, saying that people were asked to vote too often or that the small numbers at the ballot box meant citizens were just casting an unwritten ballot for the status quo. Yet as participation at the polls dropped lower and lower, these rationalizations lost their power to placate us. By the 1992 presidential election, voter anger was too evident to ignore. Ads encouraged people to vote incumbents out of office—just because they were incumbents. New laws to limit terms passed by large margins.

When people do go to the ballot box these days, they often go to vote directly on problems they feel the political system has failed to address. Citizens are using referendums for everything from limiting government spending to rewriting insurance laws. In Olympia, Washington, for example, state legislators' salaries were decided by a referendum. In Long Beach, California, people wanted a referendum on zoning ordinances. In Chicago, a referendum to limit school taxing power was proposed. In the San Gabriel Valley of California, a citizens' referendum tried to overturn a controversial redevelopment project. California's Proposition 13 on tax reform has become the symbol of a new age in politics. Although there is nothing wrong with direct balloting per se, there is reason to be alarmed by the implicit message in the referendums—that representative government has failed.

What do these symptoms tell us? They point to a widespread

public reaction against the political system itself. This reaction should not be confused with the familiar attacks on "those" politicians, or the bad bureaucracy, or the misuse of public trust, or any of the other gripes people have always had about government. At the turn of the decade, we witnessed a reaction against the political system itself, a system people saw as autonomous and beyond public control. People talked as though our democracy had been subject to a hostile takeover by alien beings. They questioned whether the average citizen even influences, much less directs, the government. Lincoln's words—"government of the people, by the people, for the people"—sound like hollow rhetoric. Even after the Clinton victory, his staff recognized, "most Americans still hate politics."[2]

Not to overstate, angry Americans are not irrational. Their anger is counterbalanced by other considerations. For instance, most people are inclined to reelect their own member of Congress even if they feel some limitation on terms is needed.[3] People still want good government. But their anger says they want more; they want good politics. That was evident in the response to the Harwood study, which was as telling as the report itself.

Barely after the report hit the wire services, the response began. Nearly a thousand articles, editorials, letters to the editor, and television shows in the United States and nine other countries commented on the study. After the first printing of twenty thousand copies quickly disappeared, a second printing had to be ordered. For weeks after the report was published, Richard Harwood was invited to scores of radio talk shows. At the end of one hour-long call-in program, twelve hundred callers were still waiting to be heard. More than a thousand inquiries about the report came from citizens' organizations, political parties, members of Congress, state legislators, mayors and city councils, departments of political science, the White House, labor unions—and the Bank of Japan.

The report, even counting the cover, was less than eighty pages long. Although its findings were not new, its conclusions obviously hit a responsive chord. As a man from Pennsylvania wrote, "Your report sounded like me talking." People seemed tired of being told, in headline after headline, that they were as dumb as fence posts—

and apathetic to boot. When people read the report and saw that others shared their hopes, not just their frustrations, they perked up their ears. Taking encouragement from what he heard, one caller to a talk show said, with some relief, that until he learned about the study, he thought he had been "dealt plumb out of the deck."

The Harwood study did not pretend to say what every American felt or believed. Even though demographically representative groups of people participated, the study could only report on what these people said. But beginning every quotation with that caveat would make for terrible reading. So this book will use a shorthand; the phrases "Americans believe or feel" or "people think" refer specifically to the people who participated in the study. However, given what the *New York Times* called the voters' ratification of the report a year later,[4] there is even more reason to believe that the citizens who spoke out in the Harwood forums were giving us insights into attitudes that are now widely shared by many Americans.

The Displaced Citizen

Of course, even angry Americans take great pride in their democratic heritage. We are proud of the extension of suffrage, the protection of individual rights, the ability to speak our minds. We identify with the values of a democratic order—freedom and justice. Despite this heritage, however, there are Americans on Main Street who question how much of a democracy we actually have. They believe we have democratic freedom, but they don't believe that "We, the People" even come close to ruling.

Hardly anyone would describe America today as James Bryce did in 1891, as a nation run by the public and its opinions: "Allowing for the differences to which the vast size of the country gives rise, the mass of the citizens may be deemed as directly the supreme power in the United States as the Assembly was at Athens or Syracuse."[5]

What happened to the American citizen? How did citizens become an endangered species, apparently easy to find in 1891 but seemingly in danger of extinction a hundred years later? People haven't become tired of being citizens, they just aren't sure that citizens count for much these days. Feelings of impotence cause them to defer to those in authority—a deference that undermines citizenship. People say "Let someone else take care of it" because they don't think that they are going to be heard. This sense of being pushed out of the political process cuts to the core of how Americans view politics. It is undeniable, and it is consistent. People have trouble believing that citizens can play a significant role in politics—they fear the system simply will not allow it. Yet Americans feel that their political isolation has been thrust upon them. It is not something that they have—nor would have—chosen for themselves. As a woman from Washington State put it, "People have gotten so disappointed that they don't want to get involved anymore. Yet, there are a lot of people who still want to act." Even uncertain of their power, few Americans have gone so far as to make an irrevocable break with politics or to have lost all will to act as citizens.

Many Americans would like very much to believe that the political system could be changed. Most don't drop out, they still hope. Yet even when they venture out to back a candidate or vote, their hope is fragile. When they elect new officeholders, they seem to be saying in effect, "We have been disappointed before, and if you let us down . . ." However they finish the sentence, it is clear their support is tentative. They believe that they are up against powerful forces in the political system that test their hope.

Driven Out by a Professional Political Class

People talk about being shut out of the political system as they would if they came home one evening to find the house locked and someone else inside wearing their clothes and eating their food. And citizens know who locked them out. They point their fingers at incumbent politicians, at campaign managers, at powerful lobbyists, and at those in the media. They see these groups as a professional political class, the rulers of an oligarchy that has replaced democracy. They think politics is now a game for the "big guns," particularly special interest organizations. Citizens are relegated to the sidelines, where they stand unable to control either the players or the rules of the game.

The Real Representatives: Lobbyists

Americans believe that the real representatives who control legislation are not the people they elect but powerful lobbyists like leaders of political action committees (PACs) and single-issue organizations. They say, "Citizens don't have a voice; lobbyists, special interests—they have a voice." Few people waste their time applying for membership in this exclusive club; they know they won't be accepted. They don't meet the qualifications of power, influence, and, above all else, money that seem to drive politics today.

What these people see happening doesn't fit with their concept of what representative government is supposed to be. "The original concept was for elected representatives to represent your interests," a woman from Des Moines started to say. Then she added, "That is no longer true. It is now whoever has the most money can hire the most lobbyists to influence representatives." People believe the influence of money has corrupted the political system: "There are too many pork barrel issues in Congress. . . . [Special interests] come to [members of Congress] saying, 'We want money.' They can find the money for them but not for others. The country should come first—before specific constituents." Nearly everyone can recall an instance when the country didn't come first, when powerful interests carried the day on some critical issue.

When people see the general interest sacrificed to a special interest, they say, "We feel helpless." When they see political action committees and lobbyists pursuing their own agendas relentlessly— at any cost—they throw up their hands and ask, "What can I do?" Citizens wonder whether citizens have the raw power necessary to effect change or make their voices heard. They note sorrowfully, "Citizens are part of a quiet group that doesn't seem to be noticed."

The enormous resources of lobbyists and power brokers make citizens feel insignificant by comparison. "How powerful is my one little vote if a PAC gave my representative $300,000?" asked a woman from Des Moines. A man from Philadelphia added, "Do you think your congressman is going to listen to you or someone who puts $10,000 to $15,000 into his war chest?" People get the impression that the whole political process is corrupt and has nothing to do with addressing the issues people care about or serving the public interest.

As these comments indicate, the people's anger at the political system is based to a large extent on the perception that money has replaced their influence as citizens and voters. Money—not the voter—"votes." This perception undermines the legitimacy of electoral politics. Campaigns may be successful, elections legally valid, and legislative bodies properly constituted. But the authority of our political institutions may be more in question than we like to recognize.

The Public versus the Media

The media generally see themselves as neutral referees who serve the public interest by keeping a critical eye on what politicians and governments do. The public, however, doesn't always share this perception. In fact, many citizens believe that the media are partly responsible for the public's distaste for politics. The way the media report on issues and the actions of government, some believe, actually pushes people farther away rather than bringing them closer to participating. In their view, coverage of issues is trivialized by sound bites and distorted by negativism. What people see on the news does not resonate with what is most valuable to them or with the realities of life as they experience it.

One man charged, "The whole idea of sound bites—getting a message across in 20 seconds—is absurd. Unfortunately," he added, "this is how most people learn about the events of the world." People regret the impact sound bites have on their ability to understand issues and the way they force public officials to interact with the public. "Politicians have to couch things in such a way that the media can understand them." Another person observed, "everything has to be brief and quotable." This emphasis on conveying short, quick pieces of information disconnects some Americans from the substance of politics. A Virginian put it this way: "The technology of the media and communications controls [politics].

It's sound bites, it's fast, it's quick. It has distanced every one of us from what's really going on, and has distanced all our political leaders from what's really going on with us, to a tremendous degree."

The distortion produced by sound bites is only one of people's complaints about the news they get. They also charge that the way issues are covered bears little resemblance to the way people encounter them in everyday life. The news presents issues in ideological or technical terms (as defined by the legislative process or by experts). Issues presented this way don't coincide with people's own experience. In a book that appeared about the same time as the Harwood report, E. J. Dionne argues that the press and the political system give the public "false issues" and "false choices."[6] According to Dionne, himself a journalist, issues presented in expert and overly polemic terms fail to connect with the practical problems people worry about.

This failure to connect can be found in both domestic and international issues. National defense, for example, was presented as an issue of whether our weapons system was technically superior to other nations' systems. People, on the other hand, tended to think of defense in broader and more human terms. That is, they worried more about "security" than "defense." "Security," unlike "defense," involves much more than weapons systems.[7]

Whenever people fail to see what they care about reflected in the coverage of politics, policy issues naturally seem less relevant. One person described his own reaction: "The [issues] which get trumped-up in the press, I don't care about, but I guess that's what sells newspapers. The health care problem, the homeless problem . . . all are diluted by this."

Even when people find issues covered in ways to which they can relate, coverage is often fleeting. A woman in Philadelphia reported, "The issues covered by the press blow over so quickly. You hear a lot about things and then they blow over." And yet, from her perspective, the issues she was concerned about remained even though the coverage ended.

Although the press may want citizens to become more engaged with issues, their coverage can have just the opposite effect— discouraging rather than encouraging greater public understanding. "It is not the media's intent, but it is certainly the result," one citizen said. As a result, people don't fully accept the media's claim that they inform the public.

Main Street Americans also dispute the media's claim to interpret events objectively. They believe the media bring a definite bias, namely, that the press gives events a decidedly "negative spin." Scouring the streets for personal scandals, badgering politicians about their personal lives, playing up arguments over small points between campaigners and among officeholders—that is the kind of coverage that troubles people. Negativism gives people more reason to avoid politics. As was pointed out in discussions on the West Coast, "We think the way that we do [about politics] because of all the negativism in the media and newspapers. We begin not to care." The same thoughts were expressed in the East: "So much negativism comes out in the media about politicians that some people figure, 'What's the use?'" People just don't want to be associated with what is always presented as "a mess."

The media, far from being on the sidelines of politics, are seen as a major political actor with tremendous power—power that makes average citizens despair of having any influence. People say, "We are at the mercy of the press." Or they complain, "[Politics] is steered by the media." People also believe that "what is reported is often different from what really happened." They say, "Things get so slanted by the media." The media are seen as deliberately trying to sway people. So citizens distrust what the media put into the marketplace of information because they are wary of the emphasis placed on issues and the consistency of the reporting.

Campaigns That Turn People Away

The time when Americans are most expected to join in politics is during election campaigns. Unfortunately, the hoopla, fiery speeches, slick ads, and other aspects of campaigns make some people more wary than ever. One citizen put it this way: "Questions do come out of campaigns. . . . People begin to ask: 'What's wrong with our system?'" The charges and countercharges give the impression that virtually everything is wrong. Americans' concerns about political campaigns are no secret: There is too much mudslinging, money has too much influence, and too few good people are involved in politics.

The skyrocketing costs of campaigning is particularly abhorrent. It reinforces the sense that money rules. Someone from Richmond, Virginia, said flatly, "My concerns are financial. It costs so much to run." He continued, "A candidate proves he's financially irresponsible by being willing to squander millions of dollars to win a $100,000-a-year job."

Of course, representatives have to raise large sums of money in order to get access to the public through the media. The irony is that these large sums of money raised to attract the people end by repelling them. Americans on Main Street see this contradiction in the political system, and it adds to their conviction that something is fundamentally wrong with politics as usual.

Out-of-control costs are not the only problem with political campaigns. The negative aspects of campaigning—witnessed especially in recent elections—steer Americans away from politics. "You always have negative images [today] of people running for office," noted one man. Do Americans believe that the electoral system produces the best leaders? No. Many believe "whoever slings the most mud wins." People may be titillated by all the negative advertising but, ultimately, they find it insulting. While negative campaigning may work for a particular candidate in the short run, the long-term price for the country is increased voter alienation.

Citizens without Representatives

Besides blaming interest group lobbyists, the media, and campaign tactics, people also blame their own representatives for pushing citizens out of the political system. When representatives stay in office for long periods, citizens doubt their representativeness. Citizens want to rely on the relationship between the elected and the electors for access to the political system. Unfortunately, however, this all-important relationship is now in serious disrepair.

Out of Touch with the Mainstream   There are a number of reasons why Americans think the representative system no longer represents them. First, people believe that officials of government are out of touch with citizens and their concerns, that they are not accessible and responsive. Officials, people say, have closeted themselves away from the public. That is a perception that, whether true or not, citizens hold to with conviction. And it fuels the drive to impose term limits.

"You can't talk to policymakers face-to-face," said one frustrated man from Pennsylvania. A woman from Virginia suggested a reason for the lack of contact today: "I think years ago politics was different. You could talk to your politician. . . . Today, the population is so big that it has distanced him from you." Another person in Iowa questioned this explanation. She wondered whether officials even wanted to be accessible to the public. Perhaps politicians on talk shows are changing this perception, but citizens in 1991 found few officials who would venture willingly into open discussions with them.

The reason that officials do not want to take the time to listen to the public, citizens believe, goes well beyond the fact that representatives are busy meeting the sundry demands of their work. Rather, citizens argue, there is a deeper and more fundamental problem: They believe that officials simply no longer care about the average American. People say, "I want representation. But they [our representatives] have stopped caring about us. They have nice homes and are content. They don't care about people anymore."

Representatives, whose days are consumed by responding to constituents and interest groups, may react with disbelief. But what people are saying is that they do not believe representatives pay attention to citizens *as citizens.* Constituent service is not the same as public access. Because people believe that representatives represent the interests of the powerful monied groups that get them elected, they easily conclude that elected officials are "out of touch with the mainstream of this country."

Communications That Don't Work Many citizens don't appear to give officials any credit at all for trying to communicate with them. People will acknowledge that some in government do try to stay in touch. However, this doesn't change their attitudes. In fact, many of the methods that officials use to reach their constituents—such as questionnaires and public meetings—are counterproductive. Furthermore, even those officials who do more than most to hear the public's voice are often accused by a cynical public of not listening to citizens' concerns. Many members of Congress, state legislators, and executives from state and local government provide numerous opportunities for citizens to participate in the policy process. Yet even when people know about these opportunities, they still believe no one is listening to what they say. Later chapters will explore this "Catch 22": Officials are damned if they don't reach out and often damned if they do.

When the official mechanisms for listening to the public—for example, opinion surveys—often make the situation worse, it is not a simple matter to reconnect citizens and officeholders. People criticize polls and questionnaires, believing that they tend to diminish rather than enlarge citizens' voices. They point to the shortcomings of opinion surveys, complaining that surveys are impersonal, that there is no room for the individual, and that respondents have no identity. By their very nature, opinion surveys are designed to segment Americans automatically and anonymously into easily identifiable groups. A Californian talked about his reaction to participating in a survey: "I did once fill out a questionnaire that [my congressman] sent out. . . . But now I figure, what good will my response do since it will be merged with 5,000 others?" Adding insult to injury, very few Americans are ever asked to answer a poll.

A woman from Seattle argued even more strenuously against the pitfalls of public opinion surveys and offered an alternative. She reasoned, "Surveys can be turned into any answer—and result—you want." Her suggestion: "Discussions help to fill in the cracks that surveys can't cover."

Letters to officials fare no better in the eyes of citizens who want to have their voices heard. People do not believe that their letters can make any difference. They believe that only vast, organized letter drives on a single issue can have an impact. "Individual letters on issues won't matter," people say flatly.

The standard public hearings that bring citizens and officials together are probably the most counterproductive mechanism of all. People report, "I have been to too many public meetings wondering if I'm wasting my time." Or they confess, "When I come home from work I think, 'Why should I attend a public meeting since it won't change anything?'" Comments like these are common. People think that hearings don't work because little hearing goes on. Officials usually make presentations or get lectured to by some outraged individual. Little two-way communication occurs. And with no feedback, people don't think they have been heard. The prevailing sense is that a decision was reached long before the hearing was scheduled.

Another reason that hearings are often counterproductive is that citizens find officials' responses evasive. Policymakers may not be ready to take a position on an issue, but citizens react by accusing them of a lack of straight talk. Comments like the following are made: "Policymakers are speaking a different language. It's one of avoidance; it's one of 'it needs further study'—something that doesn't mean anything. They can have all of these debates on television, but when the policymaker is finished talking, you still don't know where he stands."

Rather than answer questions, citizens feel that officials will dance around them by answering a question that was never asked or by attacking the individual who posed a question originally. A woman described the experience that led her to this conclusion: "In a recent debate, I hoped that the candidates would say something that would be really clear. But it turned out to be mudslinging at the other candidate. I feel like making them answer the question." So Americans get the impression that officials "give the public lip service and go their merry way."

The frustration that Americans feel concerning this dearth of "straight talk" is strong. Not only do citizens believe that officials avoid giving direct answers, but they also often wonder whether officials are even telling the truth. "[Officials] have this 'blowing in the wind' attitude, saying whatever we want them to say," one person complained. Another agreed, "They are always making promises they can't keep; I wish politicians were more honest." Someone else observed: "People have lost faith in their policymakers because they always tell what they're going to do and they never follow through. Or they stand up there and tell blatant lies—at least it seems in recent years—and make statements that you know can't be true. [For instance,] you know it's going to cost money to run a government and they tell you 'no new taxes.'"

All of this raises an interesting question: If representatives did "tell the truth," would the public reelect them? Candid candidates certainly have not fared well in some elections. In one survey, a large minority (35 percent) said that if politicians really told people what sacrifices would be necessary, citizens would rebel and vote them out of office. On the other hand, at least a numerical majority of people (around 57 percent) said that the public should support politicians who stand up for what they believe is true, even if their version of the truth is unpopular.[8]

There is one time, of course, when everyone agrees that officials really listen to the public's concerns—election time. People say officials know they need the public then. They depend on votes for their livelihood. Yet, the attention to the public so peculiar to election campaigns makes for a sharp contrast with the times when people don't see officials at all. At election time, citizens can find officials on street corners, in shopping malls, and at picnics, rubbing shoulders and talking with them. Under these circumstances, however, politicians often come across as being interested in reelection—not in representation.

Officials must fundamentally change the way they think about and interact with citizens if the citizen-official relationship is to improve. Citizens want an ongoing, give-and-take relationship with their public officials. They do not necessarily need to talk to officials face-to-face, but they seek interaction in an open and ongoing dialogue. Only a change in relationship can change deeply held perceptions.

A Matter of Self-Interest Citizens' concerns about access are only part of their worries about the people they elect to represent them. Alan Ehrenhalt, a political analyst, thinks that despite having people of more diverse backgrounds in elective office these days, our representatives have one common drive—personal ambition. They run for office not so much to serve the public as to hold the office.[9] Many citizens have come to the same conclusion.

"Do politicians run for office to help people?" someone from Los Angeles asked. "I don't think so," he said, responding to his own question. They run, he believed, to help themselves. Distrust is reflected in the almost universal perception that politicians are busy looking out for themselves and their friends. Sometimes the motives are seen as financial: "You see someone go into politics and they never come out poor." Or, "Somebody is giving them money from somewhere."

Others believe that officials, once in office, also look for ways to help their close friends and associates. "There's too much cronyism in appointments," people complain. "[The objective] is to get my compadre, my friend, my so-and-so into office." Although these may not be the perceptions that people have of their own representative, the sense that there is a self-serving political class leads people to lament, "We just feel like we have no control over our politicians."

Captives of Special Interests Who, then, has control over office-holders? To whom do they listen? Citizens have a ready answer: Officials are captives of lobbyists, political action committees, and other special interests. In Philadelphia a man said, with others nodding in agreement, "The special interests and the lobbyists are in Washington 365 days of the year. They have no trouble getting the ear of the congressmen or senators."

The lobbyists' power is, in part, the power of money. But how does money work to control the representatives? Some believe its influence is direct, that money goes into officials' pockets. Others recognize the influence of money as indirect: It controls access. That is a very sore point because the one thing that citizens feel entitled to is access—and they don't believe they have meaningful access.

As people in Seattle saw the problem, "Lobbyists who have money can say, 'Congressman, come out to lunch with me to hear my

point of view.'" The lunch table, then, becomes the forum for a
"public" debate. Officials and special interests can sit at that table,
but the public is not to be found.

Victims of Their Own Game Surprisingly, citizens believe that
they are not the only victims of a troubled political system. Officials
are also seen as victims of the very game of politics they help create.
Citizens say, with some resignation, that in order for the political system to move ahead—to produce action—backroom deals and under-
the-table agreements must be made. "Policymakers have to play the
game, scratch the next guy's back," a realist concluded. "There are
certain things that have to happen to get things done." Another person reasoned, "[Politicians] are 'surrounded' and don't have many in-
centives to battle against lobbyists. They just get encircled."

Citizens feel that officials have become caught in the web of special interests, money, and deals. As one understanding soul said, "I
think a lot of congressmen, especially the newer ones, go with our
best interests. But they get caught up in the system and eventually
just blend in." Even those who decide not to blend in, many believe, are either pushed out or leave of their own accord, frustrated
and disgusted. These same sentiments were voiced in remarks like
the following: "Many men have gone to Congress and then not
sought re-election because they are disenchanted with the power
brokers and the situation in Washington. It is not conducive to re-
taining the best people. They realize that they are totally ineffective
if they don't play the game."

The Public Interest: The Only Interest Not Represented

Citizens believe that the major forces in politics—lobbyists,
special interest organizations, expensive campaigns, political action
committees, and the media—have created an environment in which
members of the professional political class each pursue their own
interests with little regard for the common good. Sometimes these
political professionals succeed in getting their own way; at other

times they compromise among themselves. In any case, the larger public interests seem to go unrepresented and unserved. This is not the way elected officials see themselves, but it is some citizens' abiding perception of the representative system.

What these complaints about politics do not tell us is how the public sees itself. What is the public's perception of the public? Do citizens take their share of the tar and feathers they hand out so readily to others? That is the subject of the next chapter.

Notes

1. Dye and Zeigler, *The Irony of Democracy*, 2.
2. Nagourney, "Clinton Faces 'Challenges We Wanted.'"
3. Benedetto, "For Most, Political System Is Working."
4. "The Voters, Yes. But Which Ones?"
5. Bryce, *The American Commonwealth*, 257.
6. See Dionne, *Why Americans Hate Politics*.
7. Public Agenda Foundation, *The Public, the Soviets, and Nuclear Arms*.
8. Doble, "An Analysis of Results from Two Focus Groups," 20–21.
9. Ehrenhalt, *The United States of Ambition*.

2

The Struggle to Get Back In: What Responsibilities Are Citizens Willing to Take?

The way the political system excludes citizens certainly does not fit with the way people think politics should operate. So they look for a way back into the system, for a way to participate effectively. Yet the door they are looking for eludes them, and they feel lost.

Citizens are unsure of how to participate. In Dallas, a woman spoke out with more than a little frustration: "I'm never aware of an opportunity to go somewhere and express my opinion and have someone hear what I have to say. I don't have the time to sit down and write a letter. I don't even know where I would send it. I could write to the editorial page, but . . . I wonder if anyone who is in a position to make changes would read my editorial."

This woman, bewildered about how to participate in politics today, is not alone. Another person said pointedly, "If I were really upset about something, I'm not sure that I would know how to do something about it." As the testimony in the last chapter demonstrated, questionnaires, letters, and public meetings are not seen as effective ways into the system. Not even voting gives people the voice they believe they should have in politics.[1]

Why People Don't Vote

We saw a welcomed increase in voter participation in 1992: 55 percent of eligible citizens voted nationally.[2] Lest we breathe too much a sigh of relief, however, we need to remember that President Clinton's 44 percent plurality of the voters translates into an endorsement by only 24 percent of the citizenry.[3]

The problem with voting is that many people don't believe that the power is in the ballot box. They believe that it is in the cash box. Given the significant numbers of Americans who feel that money counts more than votes, the low turnout for elections shouldn't be surprising. Voting has declined for the last thirty years. At our best, the United States has lower voter turnout rates than most other democratic nations.[4] This disinclination to vote does not necessarily mean, however, that people believe the type of person elected to office, especially to the presidency, doesn't matter.[5] They just believe that the votes of individual citizens count less than other factors.

Another problem may be that voting doesn't allow citizens to express all they feel about political issues. At its best, voting is restrictive because choices are limited to "yes" or "no." Voting is confined to options that already exist; it does not allow for full political expression. What is more, fundamental political choices can't be "elected." They have to be worked out over time, through an interactive process. Voting comes later. It is the last thing people do in politics, not the first.

There is also evidence that not voting is now a way of registering disapproval of the political system. For some people, not voting is an act of protest; not voting is a vote.[6] Asked why he didn't go to the polls, a young man in California responded frankly, "I don't want to encourage them" [referring to politicians].

This kind of cynicism feeds on itself and can rise to dangerous levels. Yet even a large number of people with such attitudes does not mean that the country has turned its back on politics, or that Americans, deep down, do not want to participate. On the contrary, many Americans appear to abstain from politics. Rather than permanently walking away from politics, they refrain from participating until they believe they can make a difference. "It's more 'frustration' than 'not caring' about the system," an unhappy citizen explained. "People do care very much, but they can't see how they can do anything about changing things." Citizens make a clear distinction between not caring about the political system and being deeply frustrated at their inability to make a difference.

When people do vote, they are often drawn to the polls by clarity about the issues and by their own attachment to them. Increased voter participation in 1992 seems to have been directly related to what citizens perceived as a greater focus on issues and an ability to ask candidates about the problems that concerned them personally.[7]

Clarity comes from understanding how issues affect what people care about most. Attachment comes from not merely knowing about, but actually wrestling with, an issue, making some effort to address it. For example, in public forums when people actually work toward making a choice on a difficult policy question, they seem to learn more about the issue than when they are just told the facts. Trying to make a choice with others requires an intellectual and emotional investment that promotes attachment.[8]

The Attraction of the Politics of Protest

When people believe they have little voice in politics, even those who do participate are prone to go after immediate and self-serving objectives rather than long-term gains. They use protests to get what they think they can get. People are not always self-serving, but disappointments with politics as usual give them a rationale for getting what they want by whatever means. Dave Foreman, founder of Earth First, says he turned to radical tactics soon after a legislative defeat for the Wilderness Society, for which he was a lobbyist. He wrote: "As I loosened my tie, propped my cowboy boots up on my desk and popped the top on another Stroh's, I thought about RARE II (Roadless Area Review and Evaluation) and why it had gone so wrong. The anti-environmental side had been extreme, radical, emotional, their arguments full of holes. We had been factual, rational. We had provided more—and better—serious public comment. But we had lost."[9]

The means people often turn to are the means they see getting results. The media give the impression that those who make the loudest noise get their way. So even though people criticize special interest groups, they sometimes adopt strategies and tactics akin to those employed by the publicists and lobbyists—even strategies and tactics they believe to be corrupting politics. Being effective in the game of politics, they decide, requires a constant flurry of "protest," staging of political events, and the manipulation of the media. People say that the only time citizens might be heard is when they decide to organize into groups—as "special interests"—and angrily protest policy decisions. Even then, however, citizens feel that their views are often disregarded. This sense of impotence seems to transcend region and circumstance. People from all walks of life, rich and poor alike, complain of being ignored as citizens.

"Change can happen, people can have a voice," one citizen suggested, "but the effort has to be well orchestrated and organized." In other words, "if you get the media involved and draw attention to the problem, then you'll have a voice."

Politics seems to have almost become an immoral equivalent of war—not just battles, but never-ending conflicts in which relationships are always adversarial. People believe what many political scientists believe—that politics is only about who gets all the cookies.[10] Politics is conflict, confrontation, and contest. Citizens playing the game of adversarial politics adopt a language that connotes war. They reason, "Why can't we fight back with people? They have their lobbyists: we can gather people together until we cannot be ignored." People come to believe that they have to enter into a process of "intimidation and embarrassment and all the unpleasant things you've got to do" to get officials to act.

One consequence of thinking of politics as a war is a propensity to go to the extreme. A man in Iowa said flatly that he felt Americans had to threaten civil disobedience in order to register their views. He observed, "The human outcry when Congress wanted to vote themselves a break demonstrates that The Voice spoke, and so they backed off. The same thing happened with Social Security—The Voice spoke, and they backed off. It takes a threat of civil disobedience and a lot of phone calls and letters . . . then they hear The Voice. The other 98 percent of the time they don't hear us."

A politics of intimidation, however, is often an unattractive option. Those who say that they have to pressure officials, raise money, and manipulate the media, will add "how disappointing" or describe what they need to do as "unpleasant." Citizens are disheartened—even disgusted—that politics has been reduced to such a level.

And the politics of protest doesn't work for everyone. Less well organized or ad hoc groups of citizens and groups with broad goals rather than a single interest are aware that when they play the game of special interests, they are at a competitive disadvantage. They know that groups with inclusive goals, rather than a single issue, often have less visibility, fewer dollars, and not as many publicists as the more powerful interest groups. Consequently, even as they "play the game," people are not encouraged to believe that citizens as citizens can really get back into the system. The very concept of good citizenship seems to have atrophied because politics has taken the form it has.

The Danger of Being Soft on Citizens

But wait a minute! If citizens join the very politics they criticize, aren't they really saying to themselves, "Someone else created this mess, we aren't responsible, so we are free to do whatever works"? Isn't that what is really wrong with politics? After all, don't people ultimately get the government they deserve? Those in the media often say that they treat issues in the way they do because "that is what the public wants." Campaign managers argue that campaigns are as they are because negative campaigns work. And as for the quality of political leadership, one university president wrote bluntly, "If a society assumes its politicians are venal, stupid, or self-serving, it will attract to its public life as an ongoing self-fulfilling prophecy, the greedy, the knavish, and the dim."[11] Is the public saying to itself, implicitly if not explicitly, "The average citizens can do no wrong, the problems are someone else's fault"?

The Citizen as Victim: Are We Creating a Culture of Helplessness and Cynicism?

All the complaints about politics, and all the cynicism underlying what people say about politics, lead to the question, Have citizens allowed themselves to become victims? A culture of helplessness, which feeds on itself, appears to be at work. People interpret nearly everything that happens in the political arena cynically. For example, people even accuse those officials who genuinely try to listen of not really hearing what citizens say. If everybody believes politics is hopeless—it is.

When pressed on the subject, people will admit that their own failure to participate contributes to the culture of cynicism. As one person concluded, "I don't think you can divorce politics from the degree to which people do or don't participate in the process. . . . [When] people don't participate, it helps to create an atmosphere of cynicism."

Some Americans are also aware that the prevailing cynicism can be infectious, that a culture or mind-set can be passed along to the next generation. That is an alarming prospect. On Main Street, they worry about the values and beliefs this generation is passing along to the next. Soberly, a woman in Pennsylvania asked, "Are we telling our children that we can't have a say? Are they already turned off before they are adults?" As people begin to think about the political attitudes the next generation is developing, they stop and begin rethinking their own attitudes.

A political culture of victimization develops over a long period of time as particular political experiences become generalized into formulas about how things always work. Political cultures are the creations of characteristic ways of perceiving and interpreting the world. As people share their frustrations about politics with each other over time, these frustrations can lead to a kind of "programming" that dictates the way people perceive themselves, officials, and their problems. Gradually, people shift from actual observations of specific experiences to mind-sets that "filter" their experiences and tell them what they mean. People explain what they do as dictated by forces beyond their control. They cite specific reasons why they see things as they do and react as they do. Yet, there is a general pattern to the way they respond to a wide variety of problems and different circumstances. A habit develops of always seeing the political system as indifferent and unresponsive. So people become more than frustrated. They drop out; they become alienated; they cease to do even the things citizens are encouraged to do—such as vote. They tell one another that voting makes no difference. Helplessness becomes a self-fulfilling prophecy.

In such situations, political cultures become dysfunctional. Even diligent citizens with the best of intentions can have a difficult time overcoming a cynical culture's power. Repeatedly rebuffed, some eventually join the cynicism—blaming others around them or sinister outside forces for their fate. Cultures can also be very coercive. Those who try to act in ways a culture opposes are encouraged or pressured to conform. An optimist in a culture of pessimism is going to be challenged constantly. People caught up in such a culture cease to believe in themselves and begin to look for strong leaders who will save them. Or people turn on the leaders they have, believing they can solve all of their problems—if they only would.

Some time ago, John Dewey identified virtually all of the factors that lead to dysfunctional political cultures. People, he wrote, come to believe that they are "caught in the sweep of forces too vast to understand or master."[12] Feeling overwhelmed by problems, people may turn inward, choosing not to participate in the decision-making process. When citizens find political issues too abstract and distant from their day-to-day existence and believe that the political system doesn't seem to value what they value, they may decide that the system will never pay attention to their concerns.[13] These perceptions, when ingrained in a political culture, create almost insurmountable barriers to participation.

This is exactly the way some see the political arena today—too large and distant for individual actions to have an impact. What is more, when people define politics as warfare and think of the political system as nothing more than a battleground for powerful interest groups, their doubts about being effective participants grow even greater. They reason that individual citizens do not have access to the "weaponry" of politics. Politics is fought by the well-prepared troops drawn from the professional political classes. This point of view is not unlike that of peasants in the Middle Ages who watched armored knights clash in distant fields. The point is that when politics is seen as separate from ordinary life, a separate realm and a specialized practice, the perception itself fuels a sense of powerlessness.

Other Barriers to Citizenship

The way one generation explicitly teaches another about politics and citizenship can be just as self-defeating as the implicit lessons of a culture of helplessness and cynicism. Ironically and sadly, young people may actually learn not to be citizens. Learning the standard definition of politics as a contest among politicians, mediated by the mechanics of government, has a debilitating effect on the political education of students. In this interpretation of politics there really isn't much for citizens to do. Citizenship is typically described as though it were a spectator sport. (Remember the classes on "how a bill is passed"?) Students learn what other people do—presidents, governors, members of Congress, justices of the courts. Most young people do not expect to have these jobs. So what they really learn is that politics is a special realm, separate from them and their daily lives. Citizenship comes across as passive, as primarily watching others.[14] Even if people are taught to watch with a critical eye, the implication is still that citizens are no more than informed consumers. When young Americans come to think of civic behavior in these passive terms, exhortations about civic duty will not prompt them to be active citizens. Americans have to overcome much of what they have been taught about politics before they can become effective in politics.

Why People Become Citizens

Conventional wisdom holds that these barriers to active citizenship are insurmountable for all but a few. People have all the opportunities they need to participate in politics; they are just too busy, too self-absorbed—too "everything"—to take advantage of their opportunities. Americans have too many toys (for example, video games, cars) that occupy their free time. Others are busy just surviving. They must hold down two or three jobs to support their families. Or they have to hunt for just one job. Only a crisis, it is believed, can motivate people to become engaged in politics. Furthermore, so this argument goes, ordinary citizens are really afraid of participating in politics—they are inhibited about speaking in public and having their neighbors or employers come to know their political views.

Of course these are real disincentives. Practicing active citizenship is demanding. Becoming an active citizen requires overcoming distractions and impediments. It requires that people claim responsibility for their own political fate. But the barriers to citizenship are not insurmountable. Conventional wisdom fails to account for a powerful countermotive—a relatively untapped reservoir of civic duty in this country.

Do citizens have to have hard evidence—concrete proof—that they can have an influence? Do people have to become unselfish, rejecting their self-interest for some visionary common good? Do they have to have a strong sense of self-confidence and a feeling of efficacy before they act as citizens? Evidently not.

To argue that citizens are too busy is essentially the same as arguing that they are too apathetic. It doesn't stand up. Those who list all the obstacles to participation are the very same people who talk in eloquent and moving ways about their struggles to get back into the political system.

The standard assumption, however, is that Americans don't become citizens willingly; they have to be prodded out of their apathy and motivated to become advocates of some cause. The first part of the assumption is that people have no preexisting political concerns, and the second is that they only enter politics in order to win on some issue of self-interest. Both are questionable.

The Harwood study found that the key to civic participation for those who participated was not the certainty of control or success but the possibility of change. Americans seem to overcome the obstacles to participation when they believe that they might have an effect—that there is some opportunity to create and witness change. A sense of possibility is a powerful force for reconnecting citizens and politics.

Participants in the Harwood discussions were clear and consistent about how a sense of possibility affected their involvement in civic projects. People said that they became active when they felt they might have some influence on events. They did not believe they could—or that they wanted to—direct all the action and call all the shots. Just a sense that there was an opportunity to contribute seemed enough. People know that what they attempt may not always be successful and that the results of their efforts may not be what they had hoped. As one woman said realistically, "You just keep trying. That doesn't mean that you will win all the time."

Is this inclination to see possibility confined to those who already have a strong sense of power and efficacy? The conventional wisdom holds that only the self-confident are likely to become active citizens. Efficacy is thought to be a precondition of participation. Certainly, a sense of confidence is related to the willingness to take initiative, and certainly a sense of powerlessness is debilitating. Yet, active citizens don't necessarily begin with confidence in their ability to be successful. Part of their decision to become active may be to acquire skills and knowledge they don't have—to become efficacious.

In other words, we may choose activities based on feelings that a particular activity will help us become effective. For example, people don't choose to begin bowling because they already feel effective as bowlers. When they decide to take up bowling, they think they will learn an exercise that will make them healthier or that they will enjoy. Not knowing how to bowl doesn't stop them. Although feeling insecure and uncomfortable at first, they try anyway. The same may be true for those who get involved with a political issue or a civic project. They see a possibility that they can make a difference and a possibility that they can acquire new skills or powers as well.[15]

Nothing Will Change unless People Act

Given everything that people say is wrong with the political system, who do they believe has ultimate responsibility for addressing the ills of politics as usual? Do they expect their representatives

to be saints? Do they insist on perfect governments? Do they believe that democracy in the ideal should be in practice tomorrow?
Do people expect the political system to correct itself? No. As critical as people are of politicians, campaigns, lobbyists, and the media,
they recognize that the public has responsibilities, too; that the
public can be derelict in doing its duty; and that, ultimately, the
public has to claim its responsibilities if any fundamental changes
are to be made.

An Untapped Reservoir of Civic Duty

The conventional wisdom is clearly wrong in its propensity to
underestimate the deep sense of civic duty that lies behind all of the
complaints and cynical comments that people make. Because they
care, citizens really struggle to make a difference in a political system that seems to have little room for them.

Americans tend to be quite proud of their community and of the
nation. They want to see political change come about, and they
want to help. "I live in a city that I am very proud of, and there are
many good things about it," said a citizen of Philadelphia. "I want it
to be even better, so I go out and vote." Voters like this Philadel-
phian try various ways to subvert politics as usual—by supporting
programs that provide direct contact with candidates rather than
having the views of prospective officeholders interpreted for them
by media personalities, and by supporting term limits in hopes of
having more responsive representatives. Because people care, they
mount campaigns to "take the system back."

When discussing the subject of who is responsible for governing
the country, Americans say repeatedly that citizens have to uphold
their end of the bargain. "If something is wrong," they ask rhetori-
cally, "does that give us the excuse not to vote? How can you rationalize not voting because politicians are corrupt? All it does is make
it easy for them to remain corrupt." Another added, "I have to realize that my opinion does count—and not have the attitude that my
policymaker is hired to speak for me. I have to express my own
opinion."

Americans believe that genuine political reform has to begin not with legislation but with people. When asked about how to deal with the ills of our political system, people say such things as, "Campaign reform won't solve all of our problems"; "Legislative reforms won't do any good if policymakers aren't hearing us"; and "If you legislate a solution, people will just get around it; they always have." People reason that reform has to begin with citizens themselves, that people have to be involved. As a man from Texas put it, "Nothing will change unless people act."

These citizens from Main Street believe that only their involvement has any chance of making representative government more representative. One person confessed, "Generally speaking, the public is not very active in politics. It's like a snowball effect—you don't feel that you can have a voice; therefore, you don't participate, and you get farther and farther apart from your representative." But, he added, perhaps thinking aloud, "Maybe if more people were active, our representatives would be better."

Americans usually understand that there can be no quick fixes when they think about the fundamental dysfunctions of the political system. They certainly have no illusions about how difficult it is for citizens to become involved and make a difference—even just to make their voices heard. In Los Angeles, someone noted, "The normal person on the street has to work hard to have a voice." But those who make the extra effort earn the respect of their fellow citizens. In Philadelphia, a woman expressed her admiration this way: "I think people in our area who get the most done, work real hard to get it done. It's not the most gratifying thing and it's not going to be in the paper—but those are the people who get things done." Civic determination runs very deep in comments such as one from Richmond, where the speaker insisted, "If we say we're frustrated and not going to do anything about it, then we won't. But if we keep trying, we might make a difference."

What Helps?

Troubled by a dangerous level of public cynicism, thoughtful people naturally ask, "What is the answer?" Even though there may be no quick fix and no one answer, there have to be some remedies. Actually, there are a number of changes that can help—changes in the way that politicians, campaign managers, interest groups, and the media deal with the public. But what can and should the public do to begin claiming its own responsibilities? What will get at the systemic problems of politics?

The Public Dialogue: Where Politics Begins

Democratic politics doesn't begin in voting to create governments; it begins in the choices about what kind of community and country people want. The most basic form of politics is conversation about these choices and about what is really in the public's interest. Serious public discourse is the seedbed, the wellspring, of democratic politics because the public is the only legitimate body that can define the public's interests. The quality of democracy depends on the quality of this kind of public talk. Changing the quality of the public dialogue begins to change politics.

Talk itself draws people back into politics. Studies of even nonpolitical associations show that "the more members talk to each other, and the more talk turns to politics, the more political interest and activity is aroused."[16] In other studies, there is more evidence of the power of public conversations. As a citizen in Little Rock testified, just talking about crime with her neighbors helped her to understand the problem and become personally involved with the issue.[17]

Public talk—citizens talking together—can also provide officials with important information about which issues are priorities to citizens, what concerns need to be addressed, and what trade-offs people are willing or unwilling to make.

While Americans can be put off by the politics they see on the evening news, they can be drawn to the public discussion of issues that affect them personally. These discussions take place on buses and in coffee shops, over the kitchen table, and in public forums. People are curious about how others interpret events and think about policy questions. They want to hear from more than the politicians, the news analysts, and the experts. They want to know what the person across the lunch counter, around the water cooler, and down the street thinks.

Public dialogue is critical in forming policy because the public requires time to digest the issues. Or, you might say the public needs a gestation period in order to make up its mind. This crucial step is the least understood in the policy process. We are much more familiar with the initial stage of policy-making, when consciousness is being raised by heavy doses of publicity, and the last stage, when legislation is passed. In between, there have to be opportunities for citizens to listen, question, and test their opinions on one another. Debate, choosing up sides and scoring points, is not what people want at this time. They want respect for ambivalence and an appreciation for the gray areas in policy questions, for matters on which there is no certainty. They want to be in settings where they can learn from one another.[18]

The most helpful discussions, people have said on reflection, were those where they could explore the nature of a problem and the opinions of others—meetings where they could say to one another, "I don't have a clue to what you are talking about; can you explain?" Meetings that have drawn high marks were those in which people could hold strong opinions without "everyone always contesting what someone else said." A forum in which participants felt "we all listened to everybody else's opinion" was a forum where people said, "We all got something out of it."[19] And getting something out of a discussion is critical. Citizens have little patience with discussion for discussion's sake. Although they want an opportunity to be ambivalent, to test their own ideas, they don't want to be ambivalent forever. The public dialogue is not an end in itself; rather, it is a means to an end, to making a decision.

In these settings, people put a high premium on hearing from those who are different and have different perspectives. "When I'm undecided about something," one person said, "I seek opinions from both sides." Yet difference was not dissonance. Americans look for environments in which it is possible to "talk grown up" without people shouting at one another. They dislike polarization, saying, "I feel very strongly about things, but . . . I believe you can stand up for what you believe and support it without going to extremes."[20] People want to find connections with one another and not just further define their differences.

In their search for what might be common to all, Americans also want to open up or broaden issues that, they believe, have been artificially segmented or narrowed in the political debate. Contrary to the conventional wisdom, people do not become clear about, and attached to, issues by breaking them down into their simplest elements. People want a public dialogue that helps them see connections among issues and between specific problems and those things they have learned to value.[21]

A public dialogue is a natural home for democratic politics. It is a home that people feel forced out of and want back into. One of the possibilities people must see, before they are willing to become active citizens, is the possibility that they can have a say. As people reflect on the importance of citizens thinking about and discussing policy issues, they describe what they do as "staying educated on issues" or "talking to other people about issues." Sometimes they go to town meetings to talk; sometimes their forum is as informal as holding "'coffees' for ten or fifteen people in our homes to talk about issues." Even if they aren't sure that others will take the time to participate (citizens do have reservations about other citizens), an overwhelming majority of Americans still say that we all need to engage in frequent and regular discussions of public issues.[22]

While most of our forums are informal, these discussions have limitations. They are often cursory, inconclusive, and parochial. A serious public dialogue requires more than chance conversations. Because this dialogue is pivotal—because we are dependent on it to define the public interest—it is imperative that we expand its reach, enlarge its scope, and ensure its integrity. The erosion of the political system's legitimacy, in the eyes of the public, is serious. Reviving the party system or increasing voter participation fails to address the source of the erosion. The only way to get at the heart of the problem is for the public to define its own interest. To do that, citizens have to talk publicly about difficult choices. The public has to come to terms with the demanding questions behind any policy issue: What is really important to us? What are our real purposes? People have to talk to each other to find their answers. That is the only way the public can define the public's interest.

The Challenges

Although our first impression may be that political problems stem from what happens (or fails to happen) in legislative halls, "smoke-filled rooms," and voting booths, our difficulties actually begin at the most basic level of politics. The doorway into politics, the public dialogue, is often jammed.

Political posturing and sound bites diminish the quality of political debate. Public forums are often just lectures by some expert or authority. Perhaps worst of all, when politics is understood as no more than constant factional conflict designed to produce "winners," there is no place for serious public discussion by those who care less about who wins and more about defining common purposes. The result is that the public dialogue isn't always taken seriously by either the professional political class or people in general.

Citizens concerned about the quality of the public dialogue usually single out three problems for particular attention: the way the political agenda is set, the way policy issues are framed, and the limited opportunities for public deliberation. Each has to do with enabling the public dialogue to be truly public and allowing the public to get at the difficult choices every important issue entails.

Loss of Control over Setting the Political Agenda   People are troubled when the issues that receive the most attention from the media, political figures, pundits, and others do not reflect their true concerns. For instance, a man from Iowa said, "It's hard for me to comprehend why they make big issues out of certain things, and other issues they don't care about." A woman from Texas complained, "The issues that policymakers jump on the bandwagon and carry on about aren't really the issues that deal with mainstream people."

There appears to be a public agenda that consists of issues that people identify with as citizens and another agenda, a politics-as-usual agenda, that is different from the public's agenda. Some citizens don't believe that they have a say in setting the usual political agenda. They believe that they have lost control over it, that it is just handed down to them from on high.

Leaving the Public Dimension out of Framing Issues Even when the topics on the public's agenda are the same as those on the official agenda, there can be a problem. There is a public dimension to every issue, yet it is often missing from the way policy matters are framed and presented. For the public to relate to an issue, it has to be framed in terms of what is valuable to people in their everyday lives, not just in terms of technical considerations. Citizens want more than information—more than "just the facts." They want to know what their choices are, choices described in terms of what is valuable to them.

People are dismayed when they cannot find connections between issues as they are presented and their own concerns. For example, when talking about the federal budget deficit they ask, "How does it affect me—my life?" Trying to figure out the effects of an issue is especially difficult today because the language used to frame issues is often a foreign, expert language. This is not to suggest that officials, the media, and others should pander to the public. Quite the contrary, citizens want to understand the experts, but they have more than technical concerns. They want to know why an issue is important. What are the risks of not acting? What are the trade-offs of various options?

The point is not whether citizens—and only citizens—already know what issues are important and why they are important. The point is that Americans in city after city, state after state, feel that they tend to be left out of the way issues are framed, that their concerns are not adequately reflected in the political debate.

Often the public dimension of an issue is left out because those who control the framing of issues don't understand how the public sees the issue. In his book *Coming to Public Judgment*, Daniel Yankelovich describes the difference between presenting issues in a way that incorporates the public's perspective and presenting them from a professional or expert perspective. To illustrate these differences, or what he calls "points of departure," Yankelovich uses the issue of freedom of expression. Professional journalists define this freedom from their own frame of reference—as producers of speech. Journalists associate their freedom to express themselves with the First Amendment. They are alarmed by any indication that the public doesn't know what the First Amendment says, and when people fail to distinguish the First from the Third Amendment, they conclude that the public is "ignorant." Actually, however, the public is very supportive of the right to free speech. Yet the people's point of departure is as consumers of news—as viewers and listeners—not producers. The public believes that the First Amendment means the right to hear, to have free access to all sides of an issue.

This difference in frames of reference can lead to great misunderstandings between the professional journalist and the public. For example, when polls show that the public favors actions that regulate the media, such as strengthening the Fairness Doctrine, journalists hear an attack on the First Amendment. However, what the public believes it is doing—by voicing these opinions—is expanding citizens' opportunity to hear all sides. Clearly, as Yankelovich concludes, each side operates from a different starting point.[23] The same is true of the way in which many issues are framed. When the public dimension is missing, citizens are less inclined to join in the political debate.

Not Enough Places to Talk Together   Americans are also unhappy that the public dialogue really isn't a dialogue. People who attend forums say that they want to talk together—to hear and to be heard. They don't just want to be lectured or "addressed."[24] As has been noted, they don't care for all the jargon, statistics, and other forms of "professional speak." This "foreign" language makes it difficult for citizens to talk to citizens.

Talking together—not just talking—is the heart of a public discussion. When people talk, they learn about issues, exchange ideas, and even change their perspectives. As someone in Virginia put it, "When you hear what others have to say, your views tend to broaden." Through discussion, people begin to see beyond their private interests and find interests they have in common. They begin to develop informed judgments on issues—judgments like those, for instance, that members of a jury reach after they have deliberated together. Informed judgment provides the foundation of common purpose needed for both citizen and government action.

The public can't talk together, however, unless there are places to sit down and discuss issues. Yet, few such places exist in our country, and consequently there are not enough opportunities for real public talk. There are a great many places where people can go to complain and to advocate, to be uplifted and persuaded, but not so many places where they can talk together with those who may have different experiences and perspectives. A citizen, reflecting on a public dialogue in Indianapolis, said, "I don't often get a chance . . . to have a convivial conversation with people who disagree with me. . . . I think this used to happen a long time ago, [but] I think that this [is] not happening. [It] could be a part of . . . why we've gotten into a mess." The same complaint was echoed on the West Coast: "This country was based on the town meeting—everyone getting together, discussing his point of view; that is not happening in this country [now]."[25]

There are all kinds of substitutes for public forums, but they really don't satisfy. Mail questionnaires and such technologies as 900 numbers, where people can register their views by pressing a button on their telephone, actually diminish the citizenry's voice. In most cases, people neither learn more about issues nor about how their fellow citizens feel. These technologies, as they are used now, don't produce informed public judgment.

Neither do most of the new electronic town meetings. Those with call-ins increase outreach but not the citizen-to-citizen interaction of reasoning together. Only so many people can be heard in an hour's program, regardless of how large the viewing audience. These shows have a pseudodemocratic appeal; we see "real people" talking and, in a sense, representing us, although no one can really represent our own unique voice.

Other town meetings are vehicles that candidates now use to gain more direct, unmediated access to citizens. People don't want news commentators telling them what politicians said in some conference or in response to a panel of experts. Citizens want to ask their own questions, hear the responses, and provide their own interpretations. Fine. But all that has happened is that more Americans are getting the kind of audience with officials that before only powerful lobbyists and moneyed interests seemed to have. While a step in the direction of democracy, perhaps, these meetings provide more personal than public access. Program formats are not designed for people to reason among themselves. People usually speak separately and individually. These programs seem excellent for airing complaints, dramatizing problems, and getting plans before the citizenry. They are not, however, really town meetings. As one editorial writer noted, "A true town meeting is not a stage or a pulpit or talk show or classroom." Town meetings are conducted among equals for the purpose of making decisions.[26]

Our enthusiasm over new opportunities for expression in "town meetings" makes us forget that real town meetings were *of* towns, not just *in* them. And George III wasn't there to answer questions.

The need for places for citizens to talk together in their own forums is still as compelling as it was when Woodrow Wilson gave the country this advice in his campaign address: "We must learn . . . to meet, as our fathers did. . . . There must be discussion and debate, in which all freely participate. . . . The whole purpose of democracy is that we may hold counsel with one another. . . . For only [then] . . . can the general interests of a great people be compounded into a policy suitable to all."

Notes

1. Knoll, "Making My Vote Count by Refusing to Cast It," 49.
2. Pear, "55 Percent Voting Rate Reverses 30-Year Decline."
3. Schneider, "A Loud Vote for Change," 2,543.
4. Landers, "Why America Doesn't Vote," 82.
5. Benedetto, "Voter Unease Over-rated, 61 Percent Back Incumbents."
6. Knoll, "Making My Vote Count by Refusing to Cast It," 20.
7. Price, "Poll Says Campaign Pleased Voters."
8. Uhlaner, "Electoral Participation," 35–40.
9. Foreman, *Confessions of an Eco-Warrior,* 13.
10. See Lasswell, *Politics: Who Gets What, When, How.*
11. Giamatti, *The University and the Public Interest,* 168.
12. Dewey, *The Public and Its Problems,* 135.
13. For a more detailed description of the psychology of participation, see Stone, *The Psychology of Politics,* and Renshon, *Psychological Needs and Political Behavior.*

14. Andrain, *Children and Civic Awareness*, 24.

15. See Stone, *The Psychology of Politics*, and Renshon, *Psychological Needs*.

16. Erickson and Nosanchuk, "How a Political Association Politicizes," 209.

17. The Harwood Group, "Meaningful Chaos," 87.

18. Ibid., 67–68.

19. Ibid., 60–68.

20. Ibid., 61–65.

21. Ibid., 13–19.

22. Doble, "An Analysis of Results from Two Focus Groups," 11, 21.

23. Yankelovich, *Coming to Public Judgment*, 95–96.

24. Perry, *Citizens and Policymakers in Community Forums*, 5.

25. The Harwood Group, "Meaningful Chaos," 60, 64.

26. Campbell, "Clinton's Little Tic."

Part 2

Politics from the Politicians' Perspective

We must look beyond mere mechanical refinements of the legislative process or of the executive operation. What we need to understand more clearly is the relationship of people in a representative democracy to its government. The "citizenship gap"—that dead-air space, so to speak, that vacuum—between the people and their government . . . is a greater threat to our government and our social structure than any external threat by far.

—Hubert H. Humphrey

3

The Way Things Were
Supposed to Be

Given Americans' sense of civic duty and national pride, how could they have become so disengaged from a political system that is supposedly "of the people, by the people, for the people"? Why hasn't the system always been responsive to citizens? As one citizen wondered aloud, "Why does there have to be such a struggle for us to have a meaningful voice in a democratic country?"

We know that people feel pushed out of the system by a professional political class of lobbyists, politicians, and the media. How could these professional politicians have amassed such power? The answer is that our political system functions the way it does, in part, because it was designed that way. When citizens express their anger at representatives who shield themselves from popular opinion, and at interest groups who turn politics into a contest over who gets what, they are reacting against established norms about how politics must work.

There is no doubt that the country values democracy. Yet, we have to remember that the government was constructed to guard against what were thought to be the weaknesses of popular democracy. The current anger has its roots in the relatively weak role given citizens in the design of republican government. So more is at issue than the character or competence of this generation of political professionals—those whom people like to blame for pushing them out of the system. Long before modern interest groups were formed, before there were sound bites and big government, some

Americans worried that the political system was evolving into one that would lose touch with the average citizen and be easily corrupted by money. These Anti-federalists, so called because of their concerns about central government, feared we were creating a scheme for governing the country in which "the bulk of the people can have nothing to say to [the government]."[1] For these early patriots, the victory in the American Revolution meant an opportunity to create a political system in which self-reliant citizens managed their own affairs—not another empire where those who ruled felt little connection with the people. Such empires, it was believed, would always end in corruption, greed, and lust for power.[2] If the Anti-federalists in the eighteenth century could hear citizens two hundred years later, they might say, "We told you so!"

Our government was designed to be run by representatives. Even now, the established view is that it just wouldn't do if every citizen were directly involved in politics. The fear is that the cacophony of competing voices would be too great; we would never get anything done. So the traditional wisdom says, Work through interest groups and elected representatives; allow competition to settle differences.

The Blueprints for the United States

James Madison explained why our government operates as it does in *The Federalist Papers*, specifically in essays 10 and 51. Madison's underlying assumption was that politics brings out the worst in people—their selfishness. ("If men were angels, no government would be necessary.")[3] As Madison saw it, people would always try to use politics to further their particular interests. They would inevitably form groups or factions to secure special advantages for themselves, even if it were to the detriment of the public's interests as a whole. There would always be factions whose interests would be adverse to the "permanent and aggregate interests of the community."[4] Madison's genius, it is said, was in devising a system that uses this self-interest to control self-interests.[5] He believed that factions could not be eliminated because they were rooted in the self-interests of human beings. The only way to deal with interest groups, he reasoned, was to have so many that no one could dominate all the others. Any faction with particular interests would, in a large republic filled with many factions, be unlikely to take over because others (with opposing interests) would not allow that to happen. The agricultural faction, for example, would not be able to overpower the industrial faction. The more factions the better, so no one could get a permanent majority. The result was intended to be a good government—good in the sense that it would allow citizens the freedom to pursue their own self-interests.

The virtue of governing through interest group competition was not only that it would protect against tyranny; the competition was also seen as serving the common interest. Even if interest groups were concerned only with what benefited them, their competition would ultimately result in the government doing what was best for the country.

The notion that competition is inherently beneficial, that the "best tend to win out," came from the economic theories of Adam Smith, who developed the theory of capitalism in England at the same time that Madison developed the theory of representative government. Smith wrote that an "invisible hand" produces a superior society out of the endeavors of unfettered individual enterprise. Even if the individual parties are self-interested, the common good would be served. "Every individual . . . neither intends to promote the public interest, nor knows how much he is promoting it. . . . He intends only his own gain, and he is in this, as in many other cases, led by an invisible hand to promote an end which was no part of his intention. . . . By pursuing his own interest he frequently promotes that of the society more effectually than when he really intends to promote it."[6]

Smith's economic theory—or what was understood to be his theory—had a profound effect on the development of democratic theory. Ideas about the efficacy of self-interested competition were applied to political as well as economic behavior. Political competition was considered to be much like commercial competition. And democracy was redefined as a marketplace for free political competition. Citizens were understood to be consumers whose role was to buy, or not to buy, what interest groups were selling.

Much of today's understanding of how politics works is based on this market model. Joseph Schumpeter, a modern economist turned democratic theorist, believed democracy could be effective only if it were understood as an "institutional arrangement . . . in which individuals acquire the power to decide by means of a competitive struggle for the people's vote."[7] This kind of democracy is like intense economic competition made political. There need be few, if any, common ideals and values—only the beneficial force of political competition, the struggle for advantage. Political competition will cause the public good to be served. The best "products" (candidates and policies) will win out.

Consequently, the conventional wisdom now is that people must join interest groups if they want to participate in politics, because interest groups are the major players in the political market. By aligning with a cause, region, institution, economic interest, or profession, we can compete for our objectives through the media, through lobbying, and through the ballot box. This is perfectly democratic, because anyone can supposedly join as many groups as he or she wants. And the elusive public interests can be defined by political contests. What could be more fair?

The Case for Guardians of Democracy

The theory of representative government also made provision for leaders—elected officials who would be further safeguards against rule by the masses, officials who would put the public interest ahead of partisan interests. Although leaders could, of course, be captured by special interests, the hope was that virtuous representatives would act as trustees or guardians of what was best for all. The idea was to elect these exceptional people to positions of leadership and to rely on the best citizens to see that the "right" people were put into office and the "right" policies enacted.

Now the established view is that, at most, a very small percentage of the population, perhaps as little as 5 percent, takes the responsibility of citizenship seriously. This elite core of citizens and the people they put into office act as everyone's guardians. Those who are serious and active are opinion leaders, and they control what the masses think and do.[8] Everyone else is just along for the ride, and there is no need to pay much attention to them—except to be sure that their needs are met.

Today's arguments for guardians and against self-government are familiar. One is that self-government only works in small communities like the small city-states where it originated. America is too large to be a democracy. Another more recent claim is that our technological society is too complex for average citizens to direct. The most damning of all arguments is that Americans lack the moral character to be citizens. We are said to have lost respect for the civic values that citizens must have. We have even lost our capacity for civility. Finally, some scholars insist that the very idea of democracy is hopelessly flawed. Its principles are contrary to human nature and the nature of politics.[9] All of this leads to one conclusion: America needs guardians of the true public interest.

Those who have volunteered to serve as our guardians are often committed to a particular vision of America. They question popular rule, not because it does not lead to answers, but because it might lead to "the wrong answer." They believe guardians are needed to save America from itself. The public seems unpredictable and dangerous. So the American way of life cannot be assured by popular democracy. From this point of view, public talk is time-wasting babble—or worse. Widespread public discussion might confirm the public's deepest fears about the country's enemies and escalate conflict. So a degree of citizen indifference is essential. The public needs to be somewhat passive; if everyone were interested in everything, the political system would not work. Participation should not be overly encouraged. The danger is in having too much, not too little, public involvement in politics. Guardians see the public as a baby who, when it becomes upset, cries to alert its parental guardians. Although the "baby" public may know something is wrong, it can't provide solutions—only cry out.

Walter Lippmann gave the bluntest formulation of the case for guardians when he argued that citizens are like theatergoers who arrive in the middle of the third act and leave before the final curtain. They have neither the capacity nor the interest to direct public affairs responsibly.[10] The best citizens can do is to choose their best leaders.

To be fair to the argument for guardians, the select few are not supposed to be the most powerful but the most virtuous. They are to be the guardians of excellence in public life, practitioners of—and role models for—civic virtue. Guardian-like leaders are needed to do what is right, even in the face of popular opposition. Given the continuing fear of "the masses," support for a guardian-led republic is still around. We hear it in the often-repeated lament about the lack of strong leaders. This may seem antidemocratic, but, after all, in a republic we do get to elect our leaders. So the argument is made that our democratic ideals can be adequately realized at the ballot box. This is why there is such a premium on electoral democracy—to the exclusion of other democratic practices.

What Went Wrong?

Politics directed by the best, democratically elected leaders and mediated by the open competition of interest groups is attractive. Who could argue against leadership selected by majority vote? Who in the United States doesn't believe in the value of free competition? What is wrong with having groups champion their particular interests? Certainly there are enough groups to represent every possible interest. (Is there anything in the country for which we do not have an interest group?) How could anyone hate such a sensible political system? Yet, although people may like the theory, they don't like the results.

Was Madison wrong in his assumptions that there would always be self-interests and that it would be better to control the "mischief of factions" than to destroy liberty or try to make certain that everyone would have the same opinions? Probably not. Today we may have even more reason to believe that economic differences ("the unequal distribution of property"), ideological differences ("a zeal for different opinions"), and various ambitions for power ("different leaders ambitiously contending for preeminence and power") produce mutual animosity. We could even add racial, gender, and ethnic differences to Madison's list of the sources of conflict. Furthermore, we need to remind ourselves that Madison said the purpose of political competition was not simply to produce winners but rather to advance the public good and ensure civil rights for all.[11] And Madison believed people had the capacity ("sufficient virtue") for self-government.[12] So the point is not that Madison was wrong or that the design of our representative system is fatally flawed. It seems more profitable to look at what modern circumstances have done to the character of factions and the nature of their conflict and to consider what these forces have done to representative government.

James Madison could not have imagined what would happen in two hundred years. Yet now we know that a system of representative, faction-driven government is very vulnerable to special interest control, lobbyist manipulation, the influence of money, and thirty-second commercials. It is relatively easy to push citizens to the back of the bus—particularly if citizens help the process along by accepting their roles as consumers or by opting out of the system.

The hope that all would be made right at the ballot box is not realized when money, not votes, controls who is elected and what policies are adopted. And today's interest groups are a far cry from Madison's factions. Madison would not have believed the enormous sums of money that interest groups raise to meet the equally enormous cost of campaigns. Nor were the factions he had in mind narrow, single-issue groups. His factions were "debtors" or "landed interest" or "mercantile interests." He would not have realized that the ability to raise money to influence legislation is often greater with a single issue.

Neither could Madison have anticipated the degree to which lobbyists have become, in citizens' eyes, "the real representatives." It is quite a different matter to be represented by various lobbyists than to be represented by one person. We expect representatives to do what we do—balance carefully, give appropriate weight, and assign priorities to the various interests we have. We don't hire lobby-ists to represent our balanced views.

Interest groups are created to represent one of our particular in-terests and pressure officials to respond to one particular concern. Even if many of our interests are being advanced by various lobby-ists, we still may not feel that we (in the sense of our more integrat-ed selves) are really represented. That may be why people say that the public interest is the only interest not represented.

To be fair, interest group competition does, just as Madison hoped, keep some balance in the system. And interest group politics has its own claim to being democratic, a claim that rests on two as-sumptions. One is that everyone is in—or can be in—an interest group and can, therefore, be "represented." The other is that every-one in an interest group understands his or her interest the same way. Both assumptions, however, are questionable. Everyone in an interest group is not of the same mind. And even with all our groups, large portions of our population are not members of any "faction."[13]

Even the claim that interest groups serve to make the public more aware of issues, and of what the options are, is open to ques-tion. Certainly, interest groups serve the public good by raising citi-zens' consciousness on critical issues. They offer policy options that go beyond those offered by politicians. The problem, perhaps not of their making, is that even the interest groups may not give the public all the valid options on a policy question. All the possible "products" don't necessarily get on the shelf for citizens to consid-er. The only options the public hears, so it is charged, are those that powerful interests have decided are appropriate.[14]

Madison's assumptions about how representative government could work best have been unsettled most by what has happened to government itself in the last two hundred years. Probably the great-est change in our political circumstances since Madison's genera-tion is the far greater role that government plays in our lives. Al-though the Federalists argued for a stronger central government than was laid out in the Articles of Confederation, they still wanted only limited government. Limited government was the passion of the eighteenth century. So in that century, when government had relatively few issues to address, a clash of interests seemed tolerable. Now, however, when government affects nearly every interest and every aspect of everyday life, that clash of factions has the sound of never-ending conflict.

Politics is now consumed by government, thus changing the very nature of politics. Politics has become narrowly restricted to one task, that of managing a multitude of very large governments, state and local as well as federal. Whether that change is good or bad is not the issue here. How it has affected citizens and their role is.

To a degree, our scheme for government, with the role given to interest groups and guardians, has become a substitute for a more complete theory of politics. As government has moved to the center of the political universe, the quintessential political act has become influencing government. That is what interest groups have always done and that is how the citizens' role is defined. Consider a modern textbook's interpretation of political participation: participation is an act of *"influencing* the government, either by affecting the *choice* of government personnel or by affecting the *choices made by* government personnel."[15]

The implications of this definition are far-reaching. Citizens are not thought of as the legitimate authors of the public's interest. Instead, they are looked upon as supplicants trying to influence government on their own behalf, recruits for bringing group pressure, or consumers of the prefabricated opinions of others. The problem isn't that citizens have no role in this redefinition of politics; it is that their role demotes them from the first officers of a democracy to mere conscripts.

In this vision of politics as a special realm directed by governments and "professionals," ordinary citizens have to be drafted for political duty the way recruits are brought into an army. The idea is to make advocates of the supposedly apathetic. So "pols" enlist citizens in order to bring their influence to bear on a wide array of causes and to serve as cannon fodder for the factional warfare of interest group politics.

To increase their clout, interest groups naturally try to recruit more and more citizens. They bombard citizens with appealing images and sound bites to sell them on a particular point of view or "solution" to a political problem. Of course, this changes the character of political debate. The purpose of the exchange is not to listen to people, to open up a two-way dialogue; the objective is to persuade.

By giving government the central role and making "influencing" the essence of political activity, interest groups and guardian politicians not only turn the political debate into a sales meeting, but they also create an unusual, post-Madisonian, theory of representation. The basic unit of politics is no longer to be the individual citizen but a corporate body, a group of some type. Individuals are important only if they are represented by a group or are, themselves, representatives of a group. In a recent movie, *Roger and Me*, the principal character is denied entry into an office on the grounds that he "did not represent anyone." In that same sense, citizens as citizens don't have any standing or voice.[16] They don't represent anyone but themselves.

In this concept of representation, elected officials are presumed not to represent individuals; rather, they represent groups. The consequence is that citizens no longer feel they are represented by anyone. And in this kind of politics, they aren't.

The way modern factions and political leaders conduct politics sets a powerful example for others. Today, whether in a high school classroom or a senior citizen center, whether in a corporate boardroom or a low-income neighborhood, many believe that the only way things get done in politics is to sell the public on political solutions, the same way marketers sell the public on soap or cars. And "what is" easily becomes "what should be." Treating citizens as consumers, concentrating on telling them what is good for them, is much easier than really involving them in politics. Sitting back as a tax-paying consumer and criticizing government's guardians is much easier for people than taking the initiative themselves. And deciding matters in open factional combat has the assuring attraction of the free competition that Americans cherish. If we are honest with ourselves, we have to admit that government by factions and guardians has its appeal.

Yet, this politics-as-usual system ultimately evokes anger and contempt. Often the same people who join interest groups—and who may feel their own groups are good—become outraged when they look at the political system as a whole.

Can We Do Better Than Politics as Usual?

Despite all that has gone wrong with politics as usual, it is still the established way of doing business. Politics may not work as citizens want it to, but maybe there isn't any alternative because of people's selfish self-interest. Modern realists say, like it or not, we have to have powerful interest groups, factional conflict, and constant manipulation of the press to bring outside influence to bear on the government. Because the public is divided into factions around particular interests, the best we can hope for is open competition. Are we necessarily slaves to our own selfishness then? And if so, what are the costs of that slavery?

To make self-interest the cornerstone of our political system precludes any coherent sense of the common good, argues Benjamin Barber, a contemporary democratic theorist. Barber worries that no foundation for citizenship or civic virtue will be found in a political system based on maximizing self-interest. Politics becomes no more than "the conduct of public affairs for private advantage."[17] A democracy that operates like a marketplace for competing interests demotes politics to the regulation of passions with countervailing passions. "Modern political philosophy," the columnist George Will contends, "has transformed a fact (man's appetitive nature) into a moral principle." A society so constructed, he argues, cannot long endure because our sense of "shared fate" and duty to one another has become thin gruel.[18] Can we really believe that some "guiding hand" will produce a common good out of aggregated selfishness, that it is a substitute for a sense of shared fate and civic duty? No, say the critics; to believe that is to believe in political alchemy. After all, even Adam Smith believed that competition had to be carried on in a moral or ethical context.

What, then, could be a basis for an alternative to politics as usual? Can we assume that enough people are really unselfish and altruistic and, therefore, do away with our safeguards? Should we—can we—eliminate all kinds of interest groups? Are all interest groups promoting the narrow interest of their members? Should we expect less of our leaders than that they be dedicated to the public interest? No!

A basis for a different kind of politics is found in the Main Street study and other case studies that show that self-interest is not always selfish interest, that our interests can be broad and general, not just narrow. People have a self-interest in advancing the broader public interest.

What about the truism that we always vote our pocketbooks? At best, it is only partially true. Shared values, or what some call "macromotives," very much affect our political behavior. Moreover, successful reforms—from abolition to civil rights—have been based on widely shared values about what was thought to be in the larger public interest.[19] Of course we have differences over what is in our common interest, yet people have, and act out of, interests other than those that are narrow and particular.

Broader self-interests grow out of the varied relationships we have with other people. As the community organizer Ernesto Cortes points out, "I was born Mexican and I was born in San Antonio. Understanding my interests has to do with understanding also my history, my situation, my relationship with those people who are important to me, my children, my family, etc." The very word *interests*, he notes, refers to that which is among or between (*inter esse*), so his self-interests are constituted by those he is among and to whom he is connected.[20]

These broader interests include the community as a whole and such public goods as air and water. Common sense tells us that when a public good is threatened, we are all at risk—a hole in one end of the boat is going to bring water to the other. Repairing the boat is not an unselfish or noble act; it is simply the expression of a self-interest in something common. People can appreciate their interdependence. Ernesto Cortes explains his own sense of interdependence: "I have three children, a wife, a house. And it is in my interest, for example, for my neighborhood to be secure. It is in my interest for my child to be able to go to school without worrying about being killed. . . . So I want to do something about the schools now, not just because I'm caring about other people's kids, but because I'm caring about my own child." Cortes knew that he couldn't protect his child by himself; he couldn't stop the violence in the schools alone. He couldn't get what he wanted without someone else. So he developed an "interest" in the others who could help him, and he learned to reciprocate in helping them in order to get the assistance he needed.[21]

Like Cortes, we reason that a healthy community is in our self-interest, so we should do what is needed to help our community— even if it is difficult. For example, members of a leadership group in Montgomery, Alabama, decided that they could not have the kind of community they wanted unless they acted together to improve race relations. One member of the group said, "I think we're talking about a bunch of interconnected problems. . . . But in our city, if we had to pick one, it would have to be racism. . . . racial politics goes to the heart of so many things that we consider problems."[22]

People will act to advance the public interest on such difficult, long-term problems as race relations even when there is little immediate, personal benefit. Amitai Etzioni, a sociologist, finds evidence that even when people receive little or no tangible reward for their efforts, they make moral commitments to advance the public interest. Etzioni points out that many people vote and engage in a number of voluntary political activities despite the fact that they receive virtually no direct benefits. If immediate self-interests and a cost-benefit calculus controlled our behavior, we probably wouldn't vote at all. The cost of becoming informed on many issues and candidates, and of registering and getting to the polls, outweighs any possible direct benefit that one vote out of millions could bring. In other words, people do not act just to maximize private gain. They can act out of a sense of duty, a sense of obligation to do what is in the best interest of the whole.[23] When asked why she was involved in community politics, a woman from Seattle said, "Because it is needed—so I do it." "It is needed" is not the same as "I need it." Many of us volunteer for community activities because we sense that our community "needs it." People may not always be virtuous but that does not mean they are incapable of virtue.

In the final analysis, how people behave politically may be, in part, a function of what the political norms expect of them. A political system based on advancing the public interest may be more likely to prompt a sense of civic duty than a system based on advancing private interests.

Notes

1. Main, *The Antifederalists*, 175.
2. Ketcham, *The Anti-Federalist Papers and the Constitutional Convention Debates*, 16–17.
3. Pole, *The American Constitution For and Against*, 235.
4. Ibid., 151.
5. Stone, *Republic at Risk*, 10–11.
6. Smith, *An Inquiry into the Nature and Causes of the Wealth of Nations*, 423.
7. Schumpeter, *Capitalism, Socialism and Democracy*, 269.
8. Diggins, "From Pragmatism to Natural Law," 526–28. Diggins discusses Lippmann's view that people's thoughts and opinions are determined by the media.
9. Hale, Landy, and McWilliams, "Freedom, Civic Virtue, and the Failure of Our Constitution," 13.
10. Walter Lippmann in Rossiter and Lare, *The Essential Lippmann*, 108.
11. Pole, *The American Constitution For and Against*, 152–53, 237–38.
12. Ibid., 346.
13. Lowi, *The End of Liberalism*, 71.
14. Ibid., 96.
15. Verba and Nie, *Participation in America*, 2, emphasis in the original.
16. Laumann and Knoke, *The Organizational State*, 5–8.
17. Ambrose Bierce quoted in Barber, *Strong Democracy*, 4.
18. Will, *Statecraft as Soulcraft*, 43, 45.
19. Orren, "Beyond Self-Interest," 14, 27.
20. McAfee, "Interview with Ernesto Cortes, Jr.," 2.
21. Ibid., 23–24.
22. Rona Roberts, untitled report dated November 13, 1993 [1992], which draws upon discussions held in four communities.
23. See Etzioni, *The Moral Dimension*, ix–x.

4

We, the People;
They, the Government

Someone once said, half seriously, that the most significant moment in our history may have been when Americans stopped saying "We, the People" and began saying "They, the Government." We know a good deal about what citizens think of politicians and politics, but what about the way politicians see the public? What is their side of the story about why politics isn't what it could be?

The Great Divide

A widening gulf between "We, the People" and "They, the Government," this schism in the body politic, does not serve the public interest. Although who is "right" is open to question, who suffers is not; our country and our communities suffer. Surely we need to understand more about why citizens and officeholders have little that is positive to say about one another. Saying that the problem is good people and bad government is superficial and one-sided.

What do officeholders think about the public's distrust and criticism? That question was addressed in an earlier Harwood investigation, one that explored the way officials, in this case state and local policymakers, see the public. Although the conventional wisdom is that local officials are closer to the people and therefore have a better relationship with them, the report, *The Public's Role in the Policy Process: A View from State and Local Policymakers*, found that even local officials have great difficulty in relating to the public. Officials may want to deal with the public in more effective ways. Yet often they have neither the philosophical framework nor the practical mechanism they need to do so.[1]

Someone once described how a marriage could be troubled even though each partner lived up to his or her own image of a good mate. The problem was that neither accepted the other's definition of a good partner. So, as each one became better at doing what he or she thought was right, the more they disliked one another. That is much the sort of situation in which the public and the government find themselves. What citizens often find objectionable in officials is the very behavior that policymakers believe is the right way to do their jobs.

Officials see their role and relationship to the public in almost precisely the way the theory of representative government says they should: as guardians of the public interest. They believe that the public has an opportunity to vote them out of office if people don't like the job they are doing. Otherwise, officials feel they should be left alone to do the job they were "hired" to do. They are often as frustrated with the public as the public is with them. They find the public generally uninformed, more emotional than reasonable, and indifferent to serious problems—more inclined to drink beer and watch television entertainment than to think seriously about policy issues. Nonetheless, many officials work hard to listen to and "educate" the public.

At a conference on citizens and government, a community leader from Oklahoma and a member of Congress from Wyoming were airing their mutual frustrations. The community leader voiced the average citizen's complaint that the government doesn't pay attention to the public, and the congressman described the problem of getting more mail than anyone could reasonably be expected to read. Worst of all, he said, was the implication that the public really knew what the answers were and that officials only needed to listen more closely to avoid making so many "dumb decisions."[2] He questioned what the public brings to political decision making—other than a right to be heard. Nothing blocks the relationship between the public and government officials more than uncertainty about what the public has to offer—except endless demands and ever-changing opinions. Citizens as well as officials share that uncertainty.

As long as this question is unattended, political rhetoric in this country runs the danger of patronizing the public. Able officials and sincere citizens will continue to feel a deep sense of frustration. Officeholders will be frustrated in their attempts to convey the complexities of issues. Many will continue to despair over what they see as the public's unwillingness to grapple seriously with difficult problems. For their part, citizens will sense threats to their well-being as they continue to feel left out of crucial policy decisions. Caught between conflicting assessments and prescriptions for complex problems, many will doubt both the competence and the good faith of government's leaders.[3]

Of course, officials do not all think in any one particular way. Still, many see only two options for governing the country: let representatives, after listening to the public's concerns, exercise their own best judgment about what should be done, or let the country face the uncertainties of direct popular decision making by direct balloting on issues. Officials fix on these two alternatives because they can find no middle ground; they generally do not see any way of governing with the public. Either they can run the political system in a "professional" manner, or the country will be lost to the masses.

Officials have a particular aversion to being directed by popular whims or raw public opinion. Officeholders who respond to every jump in the public pulse get low marks from their colleagues. "You will become known as 'blowing in the wind,'" warned a mayor when speaking about those politicians who follow public opinion too closely. In their minds, officials have a simple choice to make. Either they can "lead" the public by making decisions to the best of their own abilities, or they can put a finger up, test the direction of public opinion, and follow it indiscriminately. Officials think of themselves as leaders. Said a mayor, "If you are making decisions just on [public] opinions, I have a problem. . . . I just don't see our making decisions as elected officials just on opinions. If you want to do that [get] a robot."

The public's place is in the electoral booth. "The single most important act of public participation is the election," one mayor declared with finality. That same opinion was often repeated. "In representative government," said another mayor, "[the public] elects policymakers; that's the way it is." The problem, of course, is that the public is often unwilling to vote or to have voting be the sole means of relating to people in office.

Beleaguered Public Servants

The life of a conscientious representative or official is not easy. At most local levels of government, the jobs are part-time, and people serve more out of a sense of duty than for political glory. Positions on small town councils and county commissions are usually low paying and filled with perils. Local officials share with their state and federal colleagues a host of problems that never seem to go away despite their best efforts. Whether faced with economic growth or decline, there are problems of adjustment. Streets, water systems, and the physical infrastructure have to be expanded before revenues are available, or they have to be maintained after revenues have disappeared due to closing plants and empty shopping centers. Zoning divisions are a constant battle. Education is at the top of everyone's list of immediate concerns and yet low on the attention needed for fundamental changes. Environmental issues multiply with each passing day. No one wants the landfill in his or her area. The list goes on.

Decisions turn increasingly to complex scientific or technical considerations at both local and national levels. What is a safe level of chlorine in the water? Should there be any chlorine in the water at all? What role do the wetlands play in our environment? What are we sacrificing when we develop natural areas for commercial use? Should nuclear energy supplant our dependence on crude oil? What are the pros and cons of nuclear energy? What do we really know about the spread of the AIDS virus? Is the population at large at risk? Interest groups multiply on all these issues and produce gridlocks as impenetrable as the worst traffic jams. Levels of government wrangle constantly over who has jurisdiction over what and who should pay for what.

While officials who face these problems on behalf of the public might expect some appreciation or respect, they don't often get it. Once elected, many find they become "instant SOB's." Overnight, friendly neighbors turn into outraged constituents. The press treats them with such obvious suspicion that they feel guilty until proven innocent. Although what they say is always suspect, the veracity of their critics is seldom questioned. Personal lives become an open book. Families suffer along with officeholders; their plight is greeted with an unsympathetic "it comes with the territory."

What sustains officeholders under these pressures, unless they are in politics for personal gain, is a deep conviction that they are servants of the larger public interest. They are trustees of their community or state or government. They are the guardians of the common good, the judges of public controversies. As fair arbitrators, they must be above the fray. Yet this very perception, this sense of being above the fray, is at the heart of their differences with equally conscientious citizens.

The troubled relationship between citizens and officials is even more troubled when the officials are unelected—"bureaucrats," as they are called (they prefer to call themselves "professionals"). The public seems to get angrier with them than with elected representatives. The anger seems justified because unelected officials wield great power in ways the public believes is arbitrary.

The civil servants' defense is that they are also guardians of the public interest. Their intentions are the best, and professional administration is the best. However, the public doesn't quite fit into a vision of professional government. Professionals know what the public needs; citizens are more like patients or clients. Of course, not all civil servants buy into this paradigm, but it is thrust upon them by their profession.

As a scholar of public administration, Woodrow Wilson recognized that democracy and professional civil service were potentially inimical to one another.[4] Democracy is based on the premise that what the public decides takes precedence over what administrative practice dictates. Public administration operates on just the opposite principle; sound administrative practice is the controlling consideration. Put another way, bureaucracies operate according to what they believe is good administrative procedure, not what is good democratic practice. For example, in an administrative hearing on adherence to agency rules, a citizen is presumed guilty of having violated the rule until proven innocent. Unlike regular judicial proceedings, the burden of proof is on the citizen to show that he or she was not in violation of some ordinance or rule. The tavern owner who is locked in a bitter dispute over why he can't have a sign on both his front and back doors, and the homeowner who is fined because she painted her house a shade that was not exactly the shade stipulated in the ordinance for historic homes, are just two of many Americans who have run afoul of "good administrative practice."

Encounters of the unpleasant kind can touch every aspect of a citizen's life. Bureaucracies, large and small, promulgate more rules than legislative bodies pass laws. These rules, supposedly only applications of law, appear to the public to be interpretations of law. Certainly the rules have the force of law even though they were not created by elected bodies. Although there are requirements that notice be given of the intent to create a rule, and although public hearings are held, a bureaucracy is not bound by the public response it receives. There are no provisions for open debate, as there are in legislative proceedings.

The civil servants' defense is that the vagueness of laws often forces them to interpret their intent. (Vagueness or even ambiguity is often essential to getting a law passed because these qualities mute controversy.) Furthermore, most agencies do hold public hearings or invite written comment on proposed regulations.

Some civil servants, concerned about this tension between public administration and democracy, have been strong champions of public participation. They believe that encouraging citizenship is a professional obligation.[5] The very existence of public information officers or staff to government-created advisory committees demonstrates that there are those in government who want to reach out to the public. Sad to say, however, when these "access professionals" attempt to get time to explain their work on the programs for training new civil servants, their efforts are rarely supported by their superiors. Moreover, at their best, efforts to involve citizens often grow out of a rather patronizing view of the public. As an advocate of public participation observed, "The reality is that if citizens are to be self-governing, they are going to have to be sustained, encouraged, spoon-fed, and educated about public decisions by those who know what is going on." Career public officials are at the center of this democratic experiment; indeed, in this view, they now control the experiment.[6] While well intentioned, the quotation implies that the public doesn't have anything substantive to contribute. People only need to be "educated" about what the government is doing.

How Officials See the Public

While citizens are convinced that officials pay no attention to them, officeholders, both elected and appointed, have just the opposite perception. They see themselves in constant contact with the public. One local official counted the ways: "They write you letters. They call you up [and] write to the newspapers." When they're concerned about an issue, "they let you know that very quickly." Officeholders cite letters to the editor of the newspaper, as well as letters and telephone calls they receive at their offices, as the primary ways of hearing what the public has to say.

Beyond letters and telephone calls, local officials have direct contact with constituents through chance meetings in shops, conversations on Main Street, and discussions at civic clubs. County commissioners spoke quite eloquently—and forcefully—about the importance of such interaction. Said one, "I have served for nineteen years, and I know most of my constituents. I hear from them in the supermarket." Another said, "I see people in the grocery store or at other meetings—Rotary or wherever I go—and they say things in passing so I know everything is OK."

Officials, elected ones in particular, believe that they know the public very well—perhaps better than the public knows itself. Their experiences with the public shape the way they see their jobs. Yet those experiences often leave them with an unfavorable impression of the citizenry. Many believe, like Thomas Hobbes, that if left to its own devices the public would degenerate into a war of "each against each" and "each against all." Life would be "solitary, poor, nasty, brutish, and short" because, they believe, people are neither willing to take the responsibility nor equal to the task of self-government.[7]

Uninterested

"The average citizen doesn't care one way or another about public issues. It is the nature of the beast," charged a county commissioner. Many officeholders think that citizens have too many other demands on their time—at home, in the workplace, and elsewhere—to participate in policy-making. "Most people are so involved and wrapped up in getting Johnny to school, getting Johnny fed, and getting Johnny clothed, that they really don't have or take the time to get involved," observed one state legislator. Added another legislator, "When you talk about a working mom . . . [who] has no husband at home and she has four kids, she isn't worried about the national debt. She is worried about paying the light bill this month. It is not that she is deliberately uninvolved or uneducated, but she is coping with those day-to-day issues. I see it every day."

Officials do admit, however, that citizens take the initiative to participate in the policy process when an issue directly affects them. "When the interests of people are jeopardized," a county commissioner noted, "that's when they get involved." Another commissioner observed, "Most people don't get involved until their taxes go up or it's next door to them."

People in office notice the difference between the attention they give issues and the public indifference they encounter. They count attendance at meetings and find that few citizens show up for public hearings. Citizens appear to demand a great deal from officials yet little from themselves. One county commissioner bemoaning this discrepancy said, "The public spends or invests about a tenth of what they expect their elected officials to invest." So policymakers become resigned to what they perceive as apathy. "Reality is, there are a lot of people out there who don't give a damn," argued a mayor. "They really don't want to give the time. They don't want to take the time. And you have to accept that."

Uninformed

Not only don't citizens care, some officials contend; often they don't even know what is going on. Officeholders talked repeatedly about how ignorant citizens are, of how difficult it is for them to grasp the technical and expert considerations central to complex issues. The public doesn't appear to have the facts, certainly not the facts the officials have. Yet people's ignorance, as officeholders see it, does not affect their willingness to "interfere." Officials worry that the public acts increasingly out of emotion and misunderstanding. "We have a particular danger in California," a mayor explained, "in that we have the 'initiative' route that citizens can use at the local or at the state level. We often get bills, 'initiatives,' that nobody *understands*, including the people who put them on the ballot."

In order for citizens to understand policy issues, officials say that those issues must be translated. They find it difficult, however, to simplify an issue without watering the subject down until all the substance is gone. Talking about a complex issue critical to his state's financial future, one legislator described the frustration he and other representatives have felt in dealing with the public. He said the legislature had developed a plan to address an especially difficult problem but never could get the public to understand it, despite efforts to bring citizens into the process.

These "especially difficult" issues with complex technical considerations come up quite frequently, both locally and nationally. Gerald Holton, a physicist and historian of science at Harvard University, points out that "the fates of science, technology, and society have become linked in ever more complex ways, each of the three being shaped as much by the other two as by its own dynamics. By a recent estimate, nearly half the bills before the U.S. Congress have a substantial science/technology component."[8]

A scientific society challenges democratic practice. Experts believe technological issues make it harder, if not impossible, for the public to exercise its right to participate. The average citizen is thought unable to comprehend what is happening in the technical centers of our country—unable to appreciate the impact of new technologies, which scientists believe actually direct society. Public policy on such issues may cease to be public at all, many scientists feel. Policy may no longer be subject to public control.[9]

Many officials have already reached the same conclusion. It is difficult enough for the public to understand ordinary issues; it seems impossible when the issues turn on scientific considerations. Environmental issues are just one example. As one state legislator explained, "When you are talking about an issue in nebulous, over-all, philosophical [terms], people come out and you can have a dialogue with them. But when you start talking about setting a disposal site in their neighborhood, that's a different issue!" The difference is that there are matters of science and technology involved. Officials tend to agree with the experts, believing that the issues are too complex for the public to understand. Officeholders often say it is their job to know of the "best" technical solutions and to decide matters for the public.

How Officials See Themselves

When officials think of themselves as guardians of the public interest, this self-concept informs and circumscribes what they do with the public. They believe it is part of their job to interact with the public—that is, to be open if people want to say anything—although responsiveness to the public is not necessarily their first priority. They see their real job as decision maker. As they describe their duties, "[You] spend time to delve into that issue and come up with decisions. . . . [You] listen to what people have to say, but it's your decision."

Decision makers believe they have several responsibilities—to manage, arbitrate, advocate, and educate. In each of these roles, officials think of themselves as being in charge. Ironically and unfortunately, however, these roles that officials play—even when they are performed well—can leave citizens feeling ignored or patronized.

Managers of Public Problems

"Managers" identify problems and find solutions. This role is most critical in situations where officeholders believe the problems require technical solutions, although it is a role they feel they must play in nearly all situations. A mayor explained, "You despair of educating the broad public [on these issues]. It is a matter of trying to manage how the public looks at what is going on so that you can make it happen and still survive."

The central task for managers is to bring the public along and get people to accept their ideas. This involves building broad-based support for a solution and working with the media to ensure that coverage does not sensationalize conflicts. Throughout the process, officials try to "shape" public attitudes and public involvement.

Arbiters of Competing Interests

At times, various interest groups will not be able to agree on a course of action. Competing organized interests may make conflicting claims on the government. Consequently, there is no accepted solution that can be implemented. In these situations, officials feel they should act as arbiters.

Under these circumstances, officeholders go to great lengths to hear out the various partisan camps. Their role is analogous to that of a judge who listens to all the evidence from opposing sides and then renders a verdict. The public is represented in the proceedings by interest groups, which are usually well informed and may even add valuable data to the proceedings. The public at large, however, does not have the same standing. Extensive discussions with an uninformed public are considered unnecessary, perhaps even counterproductive. Certainly, officials don't normally feel that it is their role to encourage such discussion. "I [can't] give citizens every end point [on a discussion]. I don't think that is my responsibility as an elected official," said a county commissioner. "And I don't think they elect me for that—because they expect me to know more, expect me to make intelligent decisions."

Officeholders see themselves not only as judges but also as arbiters who step in when competing interests can't reconcile their differences. Like any good arbiter, they gather all the information they can and sort through it. But in the end, they don't usually act as mediators bringing the parties into agreement; they make the final decision themselves.

As Educators

Although, as one official said, officeholders may despair of educating the whole public, they still consider a degree of public education to be part of their responsibility. Some warm to this task. "The more educated the public is on an issue, I think the easier our job is," one mayor said. A state legislator agreed, "When people are educated and aware, they are more involved." Education, however, has a special meaning for officials, and it is not the sort of education that citizens always appreciate.

Often the education is provided on an "if you want to know, I'll tell you" basis. Officeholders can be passive educators, like the county commissioner who wanted people "to pick up the phone and call me once in a while or drop me a postcard—or some type of communication, anything." Although he welcomed responses to the information he gave citizens, this commissioner was not looking for a dialogue. Communication in which information flows in only one direction is typical. There is no exchange, no meeting of the minds, although officials and citizens may even take turns "educating" each other. Most official meetings with the public are structured in ways that reinforce this one-way communication. Officials tend to sit above the audience on a dais; the public sits in rows facing them.

Educating the public, for most officeholders, really means telling citizens what needs to be done—as a teacher does when lecturing. One mayor even said, "We are teachers. We are constantly doing that." Indeed they are. And like the instruction in some classrooms, theirs is not an interactive education. The citizens' role is basically to learn, to absorb what is being taught. A county commissioner described his approach to educating the public about solid waste: "[People] have to have an education that we just create too much garbage."

Some officials, on the other hand, believe that educating the public is dangerous. As one county official put it, "What would be the purpose of trying to educate the public and have the public come in on everything you deal with every day? You, as an official, would become so frustrated because you are going to have a division of forces of people all the time."

What often draws officials into educating the public, despite their reservations, is the role they think the media play—or do not play—in public education. Local officials say that the media's lack of understanding of issues has forced them to put more emphasis on their own role as educators. They can no longer react to news; they must help shape it. That requires playing a more active role in educating the public through the media. These new responsibilities, said one city manager, have "changed the way I do my job." Indeed, officeholders feel that they must take this more active role because the public learns about policy issues through the media. And they realize that if they do not act, the media will frame the issues before they can.

All of these comments by elected and appointed officials show a group of professionals doing exactly what they believe responsible guardians of the public interest should be doing—making tough decisions and trying to manage the public's reaction. Many, perhaps a sizable majority, care about the public even if the public doesn't think so. However, most do not see a real, substantive role for the public. They recognize that the public has the ultimate authority and can vote them out of office. Beyond that, what the public could do to help them do their jobs better is an unexplored issue.

Notes

1. Harwood, *The Public's Role in the Policy Process: A View from State and Local Policymakers*, 26–27.

2. Cheney, "A Difference of Perception," 17.

3. Melville, "Introducing the National Issues Forum," 9.

4. McGregor, "The Great Paradox of Democratic Citizenship and Public Personnel Administration," 126.

5. Cooper, "Citizenship and Professionalism in Public Administration," 143–44.

6. McGregor, "The Great Paradox of Democratic Citizenship and Public Personnel Administration," 127–28.

7. Hobbes, *Leviathan*, 107.

8. Holton, "Where Is Science Taking Us?" 10.

9. Prewitt, "Scientific Illiteracy and Democratic Theory," 51.

5

When Officials Need the Public

Despite uncertainty about what the public has to offer in most situations, despite their sense that they must be in charge, despite all their reservations about the public's motivations and competence, officeholders recognize that they need the public in certain circumstances. In some situations, their professional skills, expertise, and ability to judge what is in the public interest are not enough. When the public's attention is needed to keep an issue on the political front burner, when it is clear that a dispute turns on human values rather than technicalities, when public support is not forthcoming even after citizens have been "educated," or when the governing machinery is hopelessly deadlocked by a political stalemate—then officials have a different view about the role of the public. These are situations where officials admit they need a public, a public that is more than voters or interest groups.

Still, enlisting the public, getting the active support of citizens (not just their consent) confronts officials with a real dilemma. The modern theory of politics (politics as usual) doesn't tell officials what to do when they need to work with the public. Officials struggle with an inherent tension when they need the public. Their job description tells them that they have to be in charge, to make the decisions. Yet sometimes there isn't any decision they can make to solve the problem. As one mayor acknowledged, "One of the biggest challenges is how to give people ownership of the process without losing the ability to lead."

Easy Ways of Relating to the Public

First, and most obvious, officials know they need to find out what the public is thinking. One way is to survey citizens about their needs in the way a business would survey its customers. Governments provide services and, as one county commissioner noted, "What we want from the public is for [people] to communicate to us the services that they want."

This way of relating to the public creates no dilemma over roles. Officials are still in charge; citizens are consumers. Officeholders are accustomed to helping citizens, to listening to their individual concerns. Citizens know how to respond in this type of relationship. They join in by trying to "sell" officials on their needs. "The first thing we do when we elect someone to office," said a citizen from North Carolina, "is to try to sell him something."[1]

Unfortunately, what officeholders learn about consumers doesn't tell them all they need to know about citizens. With all the available polling data and with all that they hear from constituents, officials know a great deal about *what* people think. They know far less, however, about *why* the public thinks as it does. Officials do not usually hear citizens talking to citizens, only citizens talking to officials. They don't get to find out what is truly valuable to people. This deeper insight is not readily available even though officials are surrounded by the public. As one mayor said, "I think of the public as being the kind of sea that we swim in." The challenge is that seas have shifting currents; like swimmers, officeholders cannot always tell in what direction or how swiftly those currents are moving.

Officials of government are also comfortable with the public when they can direct the way citizens react to issues. There are well-honed strategies for gaining public support for their solutions, strategies developed in the 1960s, when there was a premium on citizen participation. The idea was that if more people were consulted, they would feel better and be more supportive, although policy decisions might be unaffected by what was said. In order for disgruntled citizens to vent their concerns, officeholders first hold meetings in areas directly affected by a decision. Then they schedule meetings in other areas as a means to build support for the decision they think is best. As one city manager revealed, "A lot of times we seek community input because we're looking for folks who are quite satisfied with a decision on an issue."

Officials say this sort of meeting is important in building credibility. One mayor reported that it "gives legitimacy to the effort." These gatherings show citizens that the government is open, that it provides concerned people with the opportunity to express their views. Officeholders recognize that these occasions often attract extreme views. "But I promise you," warned a county commissioner, "that if you did not have . . . [meetings] on some of these things, you on the commissioners' court would really catch it."

Credibility is like cash in the bank; it can be drawn on in the future. As one city manager put it, "I think we also seek [public input] because it gives us credibility on *other* issues. So when the next issue comes [people] . . . may be more primed to support the government because they felt as though they were treated fairly in the first instance."

Where the Going Gets Rough

Officeholders begin to have difficulties with the public when they have to deal with citizens as more than consumers, when the public can't be "managed" or sold a solution. This occurs at both the local and national level.

When Values Are at Issue and Conflict Erupts

Bodies politic become deeply divided when people cannot agree on the ultimate purposes, outcomes, or ends they want to reach. Techniques and "how-to" answers won't work, for example, on issues that raise questions about what is fair or equitable treatment in the workplace or in the allocation of benefits. Issues of racial conflict are also among those that don't lend themselves to simple arbitration. A community faced with these issues usually splinters into a multitude of highly charged political camps. Officials cannot play Solomon and be the final arbiter.

Resolving these issues requires making basic choices. Yet these choices have become increasingly difficult for the country, as well as for many communities. As one city manager described the challenge, "The issues are real tough now. Elbowroom has gotten a lot less and we need to empower people in such a way that they have input in determining what kind of community they are going to live in—what kind of community they want built around them."

Relating to the public under these conditions isn't at all easy. Standard tactics that officials use—such as "educating" or managing the public—don't work so well. There aren't any solutions that will sell. Information is seen as partisan, not objective. "Whose facts are these?" people will ask on issues like sex education in schools or abortion.

Even discussing such issues is difficult. Partisans come to officials with already hardened positions. A state legislator explained, "Trying to get people beyond their positions to actual interests and allow them to get some stakeholding [is tough]. . . . I think when the positions get hardened and the groups are out there with a stake in *winning* their position, it is a lot more difficult to get the actual interest [in moving beyond those positions]." Under these circumstances, the attitudes or opinions of the public, as a whole, are of critical importance.

When Trade-offs Have to Be Made

Officials also recognize they need the public when "push comes to shove," when limits have to be faced, and there is no consensus on how to make the necessary trade-offs. When dealing with "either-or" questions, officeholders acknowledge there are certain choices that the public must make. Yet, because of the inherent difficulty of these trade-offs, the public seems to waffle. Consider the comments of one legislator: "In Illinois several years ago we got tough on crime. My mail ran 99 percent in favor of doing that. Everyone knew what was going to happen: we put more people behind bars. But now comes time to pay for the prisons . . . and they don't want to do it." A city manager had similar concerns: "[Managers] have to balance the need for resources, and it's tough to get citizens to that point." The problem, many officials indicate, is that they do not know how to help citizens confront and weigh trade-offs. One county commissioner worried, "We all have huge problems with jails and prisons. . . . [But] I don't have a concept that the public even understands the process of what they are asking me to do in the criminal justice arena. That is an area where we don't have that kind of reasonable exchange."

Officeholders are quite aware that issues can become particularly divisive when the public is forced to face limitations. One city manager talked about community issues as being relatively easy to discuss when the topic is whether a community needs more roads or better waste treatment. Yet, he reported, "When you get to the point of where you are going to locate whatever you're talking about, then . . . it is an entirely different issue." At that point, he observed, the issue becomes a neighborhood issue where "you lose nineteen" neighborhoods because they are no longer affected by the issue, "and you pick up the one that becomes enraged because it has been selected—against its will—as the site for a new incinerator or some other public facility such as a new road."

When the Nature of the Problem Is Unclear

Officials are most willing to admit they need public involvement in framing long-range issues. These are difficult situations because it is unclear what the issue itself really is. Still, in these cases, officeholders, who may feel they are experts on other policy questions, seem less threatened by public involvement.

The challenge in long-range issues is to define rather than act on the public interest. "What is the problem?" is the central question. Solutions usually haven't been developed to the point that all the energy goes into selling them. Of course, there is no issue on which people have no position at all. Long-term issues are simply more open for exploration. What should we do if there is global warming? What kind of community do we want by the year 2010? Those are the kinds of topics that officials feel more comfortable in discussing with the public.

Creating a sense of ownership among citizens and setting a long-term direction for the community require more public involvement. As a mayor pointed out, "If people are not invested early on, if they don't have some sort of ownership . . . it just doesn't work."

When There Is Political Gridlock

Officials of government are also prompted to look for a different way of dealing with the public when partisan differences cause the massive machinery of government to grind to a halt. Not even an imminent crisis can unlock the gears in some situations. For example, in the late 1970s, the Social Security Trust Fund, which supports millions of older Americans, was in danger of bankruptcy. Despite the fact that everyone knew of the danger and its consequences, the government could not act. Polls found the public polarized. There was no agreement on what to do. Older people were angry at the thought of any change in Social Security, even though changes might be needed to cut the cost of the program. Younger workers were appalled at the poor return on their involuntary "contributions" to a program that looked as though it might be insolvent by the time they retired. Politicians quickly discovered that proposing any solution was worse for them than proposing no solution. The issue was the proverbial hot potato. As a result, the machinery of government was deadlocked.

Deadlocks occur with increasing frequency on both the local and national level. When polarization sets in and there is no counterbalancing voice speaking the intent of the public as a whole, government officials alone are not enough to define the public interest. When an effective public voice is absent, we are left with only the voices of special interests. On issues like this, officials know they need a public that is more than interest groups and a public dialogue in which people look for a common ground for action rather than just debate their positions.

John Gardner, from his experience as secretary of the U.S. Department of Health, Education and Welfare, speaks vividly about the kind of paralysis that can occur when there is no public to define the public's interests. Politics becomes Hobbes's war of all against all. Gardner finds that our capacity to frustrate one another through noncooperation has increased dramatically: "The part can hold the whole system up for ransom." He illustrates this paralysis of government with the story of a checker player being confronted by a bystander who puts a thumb on one checker and says, "Go ahead and play, just don't touch this one." Then another bystander puts a thumb on another checker with the same warning. Then another bystander and another. Gardner concludes, "The owners of the thumbs—the interest groups—do not want to make the game unwinnable. They just don't want you to touch their particular checker."[2]

Fortunately, in the Social Security case, the government did act at almost the last minute to increase funding. Perhaps representatives heard a public voice that emerged from the partisan gridlock as that gridlock became more and more a threat to all interests. Nonpartisan public forums, at the time, suggested that although young people and senior citizens continued to have differences on the issue, they could find some common ground in the need to protect the elderly ill from the catastrophic costs of care. Young people tended to soften their opposition when they thought of having to take individual responsibility for the care of their parents.[3] Seeing this change, older citizens tended to modify their position.

Although officials usually think of "the public" as either the organized interest groups or just a mass of people, neither of these publics is any help in overcoming the kind of political gridlock the Social Security case typifies. These dilemmas challenge the widely accepted premise that the public is simply the aggregate of interest groups and that the public interest can be defined by reconciling those interests that assert themselves. Deeply rooted conflicts don't yield to arbitration, and interest group gridlock becomes permanent on some issues.[4] In these situations, if there is to be any progress, politics has to become more than a contest, an endlessly adversarial process.

Politicians understand the necessity for common ground in their political dealings with one another. When facing the prospect of gridlock within their ranks, politicians turn from politics as usual to a far less adversarial form of politics. The strongest evidence of this kind of politics comes from studies of Congress. Members of Congress are under pressure both from interest groups and the particular interests of their own states. It would be easy for them to believe that the best they can do is serve these narrow, parochial interests and forget the "big picture," the larger public interest. (That is certainly what many citizens believe—that their representatives are captives of interest groups.) Members of Congress, however, say their primary responsibility is to look after the interest of the nation as a whole. They even put that responsibility ahead of looking after the interests of their own districts.[5]

To carry out their responsibility to the public interest, politicians at both the national and local levels practice a more unitary form of democracy. Unitary democracy is not just a theory, it is an observable reality. Jane Mansbridge, a political scientist who has studied unitary democracy, describes its central characteristic as policy resolution achieved on the basis of perceived common interests rather than through a compromise, which gives equitable protection to different interests.[6] When competition and conflict become overwhelming, when even compromise is impossible, officials themselves have to find their own common interests and create a common ground. In such situations it becomes clear that the interest groups do not, in fact, represent all the interests. The sum of the interest groups' interests is not the same as "the public's interest."

The rationale for unitary democracy is the common responsibility to act in the real public interest. The term *public interest* has been dismissed by most political analysts, who find it imprecise and unscientific. Yet the idea of a public interest is real and important to many representatives. Studies of Congress, for example, show that the public interest is significant "not because of its inherent meaning, but because of its value to members of Congress."[7] Concepts such as "national interest" and "public interest" appeal to officeholders because these concepts reflect their belief that a governing body must act in the larger interest.

There are times, however, when officials cannot break out of a political gridlock by creating their own common ground. Interest groups won't allow it. When that happens, officeholders need the public to assert its common sense. Officials long to hear a public voice and find in the public enough common ground to give direction and support to government. That is why many legislators return to their districts to consult the public when people are concerned about an issue on which there is no clear sense about what should be done. The issue of what to do about the rising cost of health care, for example, has caused many members of Congress to sponsor public meetings in their states.

Experienced political leaders like Richard Bolling, the former chair of the powerful House Committee on Rules, testified to the practical importance of the public in helping the government deal with the tension between interest groups and the public's interests. He believed that the government is effective only when the public provides a mandate for action in the larger interest. Bolling's experience was that, without a broad public sense of direction and without citizens who reflect that sense, legislation becomes fragmented, piecemeal, and oriented toward special interests—creating an imbalance in the political order.[8]

The difficulty, however, is that when officials reach out to the public, it is not always there. There is no public, only a mass of people with varying opinions. There is no coherent public voice to hear. Officials in government do not seem to know how to use their own experiences in finding common ground with one another to help the public create common ground.

Frustrations in Trying to Bridge the Public-Government Divide

The citizens who complained in the Harwood interviews about ineffective communication with officials have their counterparts in officeholders who complain about barriers to communicating with the public. Just as citizens say they want to speak to their representatives and be heard, officials, at least in some circumstances, say that they really need and want to hear from the public. Still, each group stands like teenagers at their first dance, backs to the gymnasium wall, not quite sure how to approach the other party.

Meetings That Don't Work

Like most citizens, officeholders usually see little use in the standard devices for bringing the public and officeholders together. Neither likes public hearings. In the typical hearing, citizens don't feel heard and officials don't feel much is said that is worth hearing. A county officeholder confessed, "We have them [public hearings] all the time and I think they are useless." Uniformly, officeholders feel very few citizens ever attend hearings and that those who do typically have one-sided views. "I think frequently you get your vocal minority there instead of a balance of opinion," another county commissioner observed. Hearings are often structured too formally and tend toward discussions that take on an adversarial tone similar to what one finds in a court of law. "At a public hearing you are more or less on trial," a commissioner reported. "You must wear your hard hat," a mayor added.

Public forums, typically informal, open-ended discussions, are viewed in a relatively better light than formal, legally mandated hearings. They are in the public's domain. "In our area, it means that the council goes to areas outside of city hall" explained a mayor. One county commissioner summed up his attitude: "I think you accomplish more and [get] more of a variety of feelings at a forum because it is not as adversarial." Perhaps officeholders feel this way because these forums are not part of the formal governing process so the meetings can be more flexible in structure and appearance. All in all, officials say that public forums can allow for a freer exchange.

What officials don't like about some forums is that they have too little structure and degenerate into gripe sessions. Unless the discussions have a purpose and focus, just getting officials and citizens in a room together won't get them past the barriers in perceptions and expectations that separate them.

Never Finding a Genuine Public Voice

Officials trying to find the public are not only frustrated by the structure of most meetings, but their efforts to contact the people on Main Street are also blocked by those who use meetings to dramatize a particular cause or point of view.

Special interest groups quickly learn that times when officials "meet the public" are excellent opportunities to advertise their views and try to sway popular opinion. So meetings become media circuses.

Not surprisingly, officeholders do not find these situations productive. The problem is not that people have interests and express their views, but that they have their heels dug in. When talking about public commentary, one legislator lamented, "The problem is so many special interest groups capsulize [an issue], feed it back into the public's mouth and minds, and [the public] spits it right back to you. It's very seldom you get a true *public* response." Another legislator agreed, saying, "They [the citizens] may or may not know exactly what the issue is and why they are responding that way." And a third legislator concluded, "It is incumbent upon us not to assume that kind of public outcry is real public opinion because it has been orchestrated and words [have been] put in people's mouths." City managers have similar experiences; efforts to get in touch with the public are described as "risky business" because officials never know whether to expect a constructive discussion or a barrage of special interest groups berating the officials and defending their own positions.

Although the organized citizenry—the interest groups—are certainly legitimate, relating to them productively is a difficult matter. In situations where there is no agreement over what is most valuable to a community or when interest group competition deadlocks the political process, interest group intransigence is the problem. Officials don't know how to reach any other part of the citizenry. They tend not to go where people are but to have people come to them. So, primarily, only the organized attend.

Given these experiences with interest group–dominated "discussions," many officials believe there is no other public voice. "I never heard of it," said one city manager when asked whether it was possible to hear a communitywide perspective on policy issues. Although made half in jest, the comment is still revealing. Officeholders seldom hear people exploring the nature of a problem among themselves—citizens struggling with a range of options or trying to find common ground for action. When officeholders walk into the room, that kind of lateral conversation usually stops, so they have difficulty believing there is any public voice other than the voice they hear in official exchanges.

Substituting the Voice of Professional Citizens

One exception to interest group–dominated conversations is discussion with a select group of broadly focused, responsible, and dutiful citizens who serve in semiofficial capacities. These are what might be called "professional citizens"—perennial members of advisory boards or trustees of established community organizations. Sometimes referred to as the "usual suspects," these citizens are accustomed to dealing with officials and are quite willing to be treated as the public's real representatives. There is no denying their usefulness. No community could do without them. However, they are not necessarily conduits to the public at large. In fact, professional citizens are sometimes more likely to represent the officials' point of view to the public than vice versa.[9]

Officials are quite aware of such citizens and are pleased to have their support. "There are, at any moment in time, probably 1,200 to 1,300 citizens who are involved in various commissions," one city manager reported. His comment was not unique. In fact, when questions are put to officeholders about different forms of public commentary, they usually talk about the advice they get from citizen representatives on governing bodies. Talking to professional citizens, however, is not the same as engaging the public. Although established civic leaders may think they are the public, they aren't.

The only other method officeholders use is a standard public relations campaign. That, too, misses the mark because the campaigns don't reach a public; they just reach a mass of unconnected individuals. Communicating with the public becomes mass communication. Yet, as citizens' comments have already shown, being bombarded with media messages is not the same thing as communication. It is information passing or solution selling. There is little the two-way exchange that real communication requires.

Hesitancy in Taking the First Step

citizens wait for officials to create new ways for the public rnment to relate, they may wait a long time. Most of the officials interviewed in the Harwood study did not seek public comment; rather, they waited to hear from the public. As one county commissioner explained, "I might think that everybody ought to be out knocking doors down and raising cain about an issue, when, in fact, the public has to tell us whether or not that is an important issue to them. And if they don't show up, that's fine." Officeholders generally conduct hearings so the public can react to predetermined budgets or legislative proposals, or they wait until outcries on an issue are so loud that they must call a meeting.

The reason for this passivity is evident in what officials have said about the way they see their job. The reason is not that officials are uninterested in what the public thinks; they want to know what is on the public's mind. The problem, at least a large part of it, is a well-established pattern of public-government interaction. In this ritual, officeholders sit back (except at election time) and wait. Sitting back is consistent with their conception of themselves as decision makers or judges, people to whom others bring their troubles. This passivity is reinforced when officials aren't sure whether the public at large really has much to tell them. Their doors are open, and active interest groups, accustomed to taking the initiative in influencing government officials, come in. They are quite happy to interpret the public to officials. Officials oblige, accepting the array of interest groups as the public.

The Ultimate Barrier: Citizens Unwilling to Believe in Citizens

Of course, some officeholders don't sit back. They are busy between elections talking with advisory groups and holding open meetings on a regular basis. Still, even these officials are frustrated by what is surely the ultimate obstacle to better relationships: citizens who really don't believe in themselves. When officials wish there were a public voice, when they really hope for something other than what they usually hear, they are bound to be disappointed if citizens don't believe that they will have any influence. The public's perception that officials will not pay attention is widespread. Even when opportunities exist for something other than the usual exchange, citizens may not take advantage of them because of a self-fulfilling, self-defeating prophecy.

Officials are quite aware of how little citizens appreciate their own influence. As one mayor reported, "There is a general cynicism about the worth of one ounce of participation in our city . . . a general feeling of 'what good does it do for me to give up something else, to go to city hall, or take some sort of citizen action in my neighborhood, because they are going to do what they want anyway.'" Another mayor lamented, "Most members of the public don't appreciate the power of their suggestions." These feelings keep Main Street citizens away from open doors. Knowing of this powerful and pervasive distrust, officials are pushed even farther into their own version of the why-bother syndrome, and a vicious cycle develops.

What Might Help

Citizens and officeholders need to say, "We've got to stop meeting like this." Many meetings preclude any improvement in relations. Officials come with their hard hats on, expecting to be beaten around the head and ears, and are seldom disappointed. The worst habits have grown up around formal hearings and open meetings. Nothing will change unless special situations are created where people can be free to step outside their usual roles. Expectations will have to be revised on both sides so that old habits—bad habits—don't control the way people interact. For instance, the public will have to let officials listen and not demand instant answers.

New types of meetings can be created by adopting new rules for the way citizens and officeholders come together. These rules are really mutual agreements between parties that need a different environment in which to work. Some rules that have been helpful in certain situations are:[10]

- Meetings are jointly convened by the parties (citizens and officials).
- No one can set preconditions on the attendance of another.

(No one can say we will only participate if the other party does thus and so.)

• Each person who attends represents only himself or herself. No one comes as a representative of a group or in an official capacity. No one presumes to speak for anyone else.

• All parties have to agree that the purpose of the meetings is not to reach agreements or a consensus but to identify possibilities, options, and new ideas.

• Discussions are open to the press, but comments are not for attribution (otherwise people are not free to be candid or to experiment).

The purpose of calling time-out, for creating a special setting, is to produce a new agreement or covenant between citizens and officeholders on how they will work together on future issues. Here are some ways these relationships might be restructured:

1. Focus on those issues and situations (described earlier) in which officials can't just "manage" the public, issues, for example, in which there is paralyzing gridlock or a lack of public consensus.

2. Start at the beginning of the process with framing or reframing issues in terms that reflect what the public considers most valuable, not in expert terms. Waiting until solutions have been agreed upon before engaging the public reinforces the widespread impression that consulting with citizens is just window dressing.

3. Insist that the public do its job, that it deliberate seriously and face the hard choices about purpose or direction that every policy requires. Do not let meetings with officeholders or question-and-answer sessions substitute for the public reasoning with itself. Create more opportunities (structured forums) for widespread public talk.

4. Use public forums to add what is all too often lacking in the political debate, a public voice. A public forum can provide valuable information not only on what people think but also on

why—information that officials can't get from polls or experts or interest groups.

The last recommendation needs more explanation. What is a "public voice"? The phrase, as used here, means more than the voice of the public. A public voice is the voice that emerges from structured forums or serious public dialogue. It is most like the voice of the jury foreman who tells the press, after a trial is over, how the jury reached its verdict. That is, a public voice describes the way citizens see an issue, how they evaluate the pros and cons of the various options (what is most valuable to them) and any common sense of purpose or direction that emerges. Unlike the outcome of a jury, it is more a description of a shared struggle than a declaration of agreements. It is not the voice of a majority but the voice of a synthesis. A public voice captures the complexity of an issue and the nuances in people's responses. For example, a public voice might show what people liked most about the option they favored least and vice versa. A public voice reflects the tone and texture of a public's attitudes.

These suggestions for a different way for citizens and officials to relate assume that people will be able to get out of their accustomed roles, that officeholders will take the risk of going into uncharted waters with citizens. The question, of course, is, Will they? Some already have.

Case studies are now appearing on alternatives to the customary hearing process. In the Twin Cities of Minnesota, the Metropolitan Council Task Force experimented with a number of small public meetings at different sites over a relatively long period. The discussions were described as "gathering perspectives" and seem to have come well in advance of reaching a decision on the issue, selecting the site for a new airport. The exercise could also be described as political mapping in which citizens and officeholders set themselves two common tasks, identifying all the self-interests and determining the norms and power dynamics at play.[11]

In St. Joseph, Missouri, in another case, Mayor Glenda Kelly and the city manager, Patt Lilly, were involved in an experiment to reframe issues in public terms. They decided to work on a health-care issue and began with a series of public meetings to find out how people experienced the problem and how they talked about it. When St. Joseph's city council had held open meetings previously, it encountered a number of problems: organized interests dominated the proceedings, discussions turned into gripe sessions, or officials and citizens described issues in such different terms that they were unable to communicate effectively. So Mayor Kelly and Patt Lilly restructured the meetings with the help of ten citizen partners. Their first task was to involve health-care professionals—without having experts dominate the framing of the issue. Like all experiments, this one has had its rough moments, but it is clearly a step in a new direction.[12]

It is too early to tell what the long-term effect of such ventures will be, but these experiments are encouraging. Although there may not be a perfect way for citizens and the government to relate, there certainly are better ways.

Notes

1. Personal communication with Terry Hutchins, director of the Public Policy Institute, Pembroke State University, Pembroke, N.C.

2. Gardner, *Toward a Pluralistic but Coherent Society*, 14.

3. Melville, *The Domestic Policy Association: A Report on Its First Year*, 21.

4. Maass, *Congress and the Common Good*, 5.

5. Vogler and Waldman, *Congress and Democracy*, 49. The authors cite a 1977 survey in which House members were asked whether they "should be primarily concerned with looking after the needs and interests of '[their] own district' or 'the nation as a whole.'" Forty-five percent responded that their primary concern was for the national interest.

6. Mansbridge, *Beyond Adversary Democracy*, 3–7.

7. Vogler and Waldman, *Congress and Democracy*, 12.

8. See Bolling, "Statement before the Committee on Governmental Affairs of the U.S. Senate."

9. Wilder and Perry, "Hard Talk Discussion Group Report," 4.

10. See Saunders and Chufrin, "A Public Peace Process." These rules evolved out of three decades of unofficial exchanges between Americans and Russians in the Dartmouth Conferences.

11. Breuer, ed., *Teaching Politics*, 32–33.

12. The Harwood Group, "The Public-Government Disconnection Project: Project Objectives," "The Public-Government Disconnection Project: St. Joseph Action Research Field Notes, September 4, 1992," and "The Public-Government Disconnection Project: St. Joseph Action Research Field Notes, October 28–29, 1992."

Part 3

A Forgotten History

Time has been given for the whole People, maturely to consider the great Question of Independence and to ripen their Judgments, dissipate their Fears, and allure their Hopes, by discussing it in News Papers and Pamphletts, by debating it, in Assemblies, Conventions, Committees of Safety and Inspection, in Town and County Meetings, as well as in private Conversations, so that the whole People in every Colony of the 13, have now adopted it, as their own Act.—This will cement the Union, and avoid those Heats and perhaps Convulsions which might have been occasioned, by such a Declaration Six Months ago.

—John Adams

6

Something Is Missing
in Politics as Usual

Ideas like government through representatives, open competition among interest groups, and voting as a means of holding officials accountable are very much a part of American politics. Yet these are not the only ideas Americans have about what should happen in politics. Something has been left out of the modern formula for politics. Representatives and other officials recognize that the formula is incomplete when they see the massive machinery of government shut down by special-interest gridlock. Citizens are even more convinced that politics is not as it should be.

What is missing in the conventional wisdom about politics? In a word, it is a concept of the public. And it is places where a mass of people can become a public and develop a genuine public voice.

Our elaborate political machinery often seems unable to deal with the problems that invade our lives and trouble us. Time and time again, the right solution eludes us. Or a solution suddenly presented by the "powers that be" seems so obviously wrongheaded that people doubt the competency and even the sanity of those making the decisions. Somewhere en route from the Greek polis to the British hustings to the New England town meeting to the airwaves of the twentieth century—somewhere along the way, we seem to have lost the occasions in which people come together as a public and define the public interest in a way that gives direction to government and common purpose to public actions. We have a people (more than 256 million of them) and governments (not only in Washington, but also in every one of our states and cities and communities). Yet, sometimes it seems as though our governments are too complex for the diverse American people to handle. Or, perhaps, the American people are too complex for their governments to handle.

As citizens struggle to find a place in politics—and as officials struggle to find the public—both may be recalling that there is more to the American tradition of politics than representative government and factional competition. There is another part of our tradition, deeply rooted in our national experience, in which the role of the citizen is as critical as—and complementary to—the role of government. There is a tradition of public politics in which the public and the government have an interdependent relationship. The case to be made in this chapter is that there are certain things that a democratic public must do in order for a representative government to work. This is the "missing link" of politics, the idea that connects democratic politics with representative government. It is an idea that needs to be revisited.

The Other American Political Tradition

Long before we devised a national system of representative government, Americans had developed a distinctive political system. Remember that we had a country for 150 years before we had a Constitution. And we governed ourselves through institutions more basic than parliaments and executive councils.

In her study comparing the French and the American Revolutions, the philosopher Hannah Arendt asked why one produced a democracy and the other a Napoleonic dictatorship.[1] Citing John Adams, Arendt maintained that the American Revolution took a different turn because the American public laid the basis not just for a revolution but for a new form of politics. She quotes Adams as saying: "'The revolution was effected before the war commenced,' not because of any specifically revolutionary or rebellious spirit but because the inhabitants of the colonies were 'formed by law into corporations, or bodies politic,' and possessed 'the right to assemble . . . in their town halls, there to deliberate upon the public affairs'; it was 'in these assemblies of towns or districts that the sentiments of the people were formed in the first place.'"[2] Arendt believed that most Americans, with the exception of Thomas Jefferson and a few others, did not fully appreciate the role the public played in creating the nation.

There are many ways of writing the history of our country's political origins. Some would begin with the explorers, others with colonization. Most would cite the Declaration of Independence, or the American Revolution, or the drafting and ratification of the Constitution. What follows is a different story, one that describes the public, or pregovernmental, origins of our political system. And it is just that—a story, an interpretation of our history. It reminds us that our nation was created by the public, not by the government.

In the Beginning: The Public

This story does not begin in 1776 or 1787 but in 1633. And the father of our country in this story is not George Washington. It is a lesser-known citizen, John Maverick, whose name appeared on a warrant calling for a meeting about a village fence.

What is now the United States was founded in October 1633 in Dorchester, Massachusetts, just outside Boston. Dorchester has a grassy plain running down to the bay. It must have been an excellent place for livestock to graze. As often happens, and must have happened then, the animals went through the fences and onto the village green. That led to two problems: first, how to protect the green; and second—the issue behind the issue—how to decide how to protect the green. In Dorchester in 1633, there was no local government to address such problems. There was not even an established forum for discussing public matters. The only gatherings were in the church, and Sunday services were not the place to discuss such worldly matters as cows and goats.[3]

At this point, John Maverick, a minister, intervened. His words were not recorded, although we can imagine him saying, "We have a problem. We need to talk about it. Let's meet on Monday." In school we are taught stirring phrases such as "Give me liberty or give me death." But John Maverick's observation—"We have a problem; let's talk about it"—should go down in history as the quintessential American political speech. Nearly every American has heard it and said it at one time or another.

The incident that created the first town meeting established a political tradition. Colonists began to meet every month, not just when the cows got out. The Dorchester gathering led to an institution that became a foundation of America's political system: the town meeting. These, however, were not at all like today's town meetings, where officials call meetings to speak and sometimes answer questions. They were forums for public dialogue and occasions in which people could reflect on and, to use Adams's word, "maturely" consider the great questions of the day.

The colonists did not adopt (as might have been expected) the English municipal form of government. Instead, they ran the colony by these town meetings or "civil bodies politik." The meetings had no authority behind them other than the power that came from the mutual promises that people made to one another, in public, to work together. These mutual promises or covenants were the bonds that held the colony together and the basis for its common endeavors.[4]

From the beginning, these meetings had a relatively democratic cast to them. For their time, they were inclusive in that participation was not limited to those eligible to vote in elections of representatives of government. Voting eligibility in the seventeenth century was quite restricted; the town meetings, on the other hand, were more open. Property ownership, for example, was not an absolute prerequisite for inclusion; even common debtors and laborers often participated.[5] Most important, the town meetings did not deal exclusively with problems of micromanagement—as in the uses of the village green. They served more basic public purposes. They were forums in which people defined their common, shared interests.[6]

This is not to say that the town meetings were perfect. Attendance was sometimes poor. They did not necessarily set a standard for freedom of expression in the colonies. Dissenters like Roger

Williams and Anne Hutchinson were banished. The town meetings reflected the character of the Puritan communities in which they took place.[7]

What is important is that the meetings began not as formal institutions of the colonial government but as public institutions. The difference between the public and the government can be seen in the conflicts between the two. The complaint of William Shirley, colonial governor of Massachusetts from 1731 to 1760, is a good illustration. With irritation he wrote that a Boston town might call a meeting: "Upon the Petition of ten of the meanest Inhabitants, who by their constant attendance there generally are the majority and outvote the Gentlemen, Merchants, Substantial Traders, and all the better part of the Inhabitants; to whom it is Irksome to attend at such meetings."[8]

These days, people ask whether government officials pay any attention to public meetings. It is clear from Governor Shirley's irritation that the first officials paid a great deal of attention. Early officials regarded the town gatherings as so important that they tried to suppress them. Despite their efforts, perhaps even because of them, town meetings and their tradition of public discussion survived— and for good reason. In Boston, the town meeting was the only legal forum people had for expressing their views.[9]

Throughout the colonies, town meetings also served another important purpose. They developed a new kind of leadership that later would be essential to the Revolution and to the framing of the Constitution. Schooled in the principles of town meeting democracy, such leaders as Samuel Adams and John Adams emerged to take the reins of a new nation. And imbued with strongly civic-minded views, everyone who participated in the town meetings (not just the famous) contributed to the American tradition of public talk.

The Revolution and the Constitution

Citizens and public bodies continued their influence throughout the revolutionary and constitutional eras. In time, the towns in Massachusetts and other colonies became a network for political action. This network was formalized in 1772, when Samuel Adams established a twenty-one-member "committee of correspondence" to create ties to other towns and explain the colonists' position "to the world." The practice was so appealing that within fifteen months all but two of the colonies had established their own committees of correspondence. In this way, the tradition of talk in the town meetings grew even stronger. And the practice of uniting the small towns, and drawing authority from the people through them, set a powerful political precedent.[10]

By the time of the American Revolution, public debate, as reflected in the Congress of 1776, turned to the question of whether a war for independence could be successful against what was then the world's greatest power. John Adams, from the town meetings of Braintree, took on the task of defending the proposed declaration. Adams's faith in the Revolution was grounded in what he had learned about people and the power of their public forums. To those who feared failure in the Revolution he replied: "But we shall not fail. The cause will raise up armies; the cause will create navies. The people, the people, if we are true to them, will carry us, and will carry themselves, gloriously, through this struggle. I care not how fickle other people have been found. I know the people of these Colonies."[11]

It was this tradition of town meetings that prompted Thomas Jefferson to declare that "the vigour given to our revolution in its commencement" had been rooted in "little republics." He believed that these little republics had "thrown the whole nation into energetic action."[12] Public talk in these forums also provided needed time for deliberation and reflection, which—as John told his wife, Abigail—were much-needed antidotes to hasty reactions.

After waging war for independence, the former colonists began writing the documents of self-government. If the king were no longer the authority for the government, who was? The same town meetings that had played such a decisive role in the Revolution had a very clear answer to that question: The people of the town meetings were in charge.

The continuing power of these meetings is clearly seen in the history of the Massachusetts Constitution, a precursor to the U.S.

Constitution. After the Revolution, the Massachusetts general court attempted to write a constitution for the state. But the people in the town meetings rejected it, sending it back. Only after it was redrafted and debated in the meetings, literally line by line, did the people of the state adopt it.[13] There were discussions and votes at every step, not only on whether the proposed constitution was valid, but also on whether the general court should have the authority to draft it. The people came together and decided what powers they wanted government to have.[14] Their actions gave validity to Thomas Paine's observation that "a constitution is not the act of a government, but of a people constituting a government."[15]

The role of extended public deliberation in constitution making is crucial. Consider the host of supposedly democratic constitutions that were written in Europe and in former colonial domains after World War I. However much these new constitutions resembled the U.S. Constitution, however expert they were in detail, they were nonetheless imposed by governments. They had not emerged from the rough-and-tumble of serious public scrutiny, and they produced relatively weak democracies.[16]

The strength of the town meetings became the strength of the U.S. Constitution. The town meetings influenced a national constitution that was unique among democratic constitutions in that it was created by talk. When the Bill of Rights was added, it explicitly protected talk—in the right to assemble and speak freely.

Little Republics and the Big Republic: A Necessary Relationship

The public's anger at being shut out of the political system today raises a question that the Constitution leaves open. While recognizing the power of the public as sovereign, the Constitution doesn't say how the public is to inform its sovereign discretion or express itself (except, of course, by voting). A constitution's recognition of the people's sovereignty becomes an abstraction if people have no opportunity to learn to exercise their sovereign rights fully. Thomas Jefferson, sensitive to this omission, encouraged the spread of town meetings through what he called the ward system: "The voice of the whole people would be thus fairly, fully, and peaceably expressed, discussed, and decided by the common reason of the society. If this avenue be shut to the call of sufferance, it will make itself heard through that of force, and we shall go on, as other nations are doing, in the endless circle of oppression, rebellion, reformation."[17] Jefferson understood that without places for the public to define its interest and create a public voice, the government could not govern effectively.

Some think of the adoption of the Constitution as the end of citizen politics and the beginning of big, representative government. But perhaps little republics and the big republic are not opposites; perhaps they are interdependent. Americans may have combined, in practice, two types of government that appear contradictory in theory, citizen democracy and representative government.[18]

The Town Meeting Tradition

Although the New England town meetings did not survive as the principal means of governing, the tradition of public assemblies did survive in a thousand different kinds of forums that spread throughout the country. Since 1787, they have helped keep our constitutional system alive by keeping the public dialogue alive. Participants in the Harwood discussions referred to their experiences in the modern descendants of the town meetings—forums, study circles, and coffees with neighbors. Town meeting democracy is no museum piece. In 1991, when the United States was engaged in war in the Middle East, the country was one large forum. And when citizens comment now on the importance of meeting with others to discuss issues, they are reflecting our country's rich tradition of public assembly and discussion. The force of the tradition may not be as strong as it should be, but it is there.

Public forums have taken various forms over time and served a variety of purposes. Their history is recalled in Leonard P. Oliver's *The Art of Citizenship*, and the following account of that history is drawn from Oliver's book. In the 1800s, Josiah Holbrook created the lyceum movement, a systematic effort to use the town meetings for civic education. After the Civil War, the Reverend John Vincent established Chautauqua programs, which brought public lectures on critical issues, plus entertainment, to pretelevision America. The formal presentations may not have been the same thing as deliberative public talk, but the idea was to stimulate and inform the dialogue. In the Progressive Era, state universities took responsibility for civic and agricultural education and, for those purposes, convened the public. Almost simultaneously, the Great Depression triggered two national forum movements: the Studebaker Forums (1932–40) and the U.S. Department of Agriculture's "Schools of Philosophy," or Farmer Discussion Forums (1935–40).[19]

Before World War II, NBC radio began the national "America's Town Meeting of the Air." Topics ranged from the relative merits of democracy, fascism, and socialism to the issue of crime. The program's objective, according to its originator, George Denny, was to get neighbors to listen to each other in a nation that had grown "citified" and "industrialized." Listeners rallied to Denny's call to revitalize American democracy in order to face the growing threat from fallen democracies in Germany and Italy.[20]

A remarkably enthusiastic response from one listener is testimony to how captivating the programs were: "Boy oh Boy! That 'Capitalism vs. Cooperativism' was a hummer! The best yet! My quiet study was just thick with flying fur—and I liked it. . . . Please send me copies of the addresses of the evening of January 9th and buy the George Washington Bridge with the balance of the enclosed dollar."[21]

More recently, forums have been used to promote general citizenship education. During the civil rights movement, public meetings to encourage voter registration gave rise to schools for citizenship. The citizenship schools developed local leadership and increased black voter turnout in the South. Soon the schools became more than voter-registration classes; they became forums where the responsibilities and values of citizenship were discussed. Also in the early 1950s, the American Library Association promoted forums through its American Heritage Project.

The American tradition of public forums still prompts people to search for places to "reason together." The Foreign Policy Association and the League of Women Voters are just two of the national organizations that now sponsor public discussions of major issues. The Foreign Policy Association regularly prepares guides for discussions of international issues. The League of Women Voters is well known for promoting voter education through discussion and for sponsoring presidential debates.

In 1981, a group of civic and educational organizations that were already sponsoring their own forums on different topics agreed to coordinate their efforts and hold some of their forums on the same policy issues. These forums on common issues became known as National Issues Forums (NIF). Each year since 1981, three policy questions of widespread national concern are selected by the participating organizations. The Kettering and the Public Agenda Foundations, both nonpartisan research foundations, prepare issue books, and local organizations provide administrative and financial support for their own forums.

When institutions began holding NIF discussions, they shared one central objective: They were decidedly not interested in just making improvements in what they were already doing—providing informative discussions. They wanted to develop a different type of public forum, one that would deal with issues from the public's perspective. That meant going behind technical, ideological, and legislative positions to find out how each issue affects what is most valuable to people. Issues are then reframed into three or four options that capture these "values" or the deeper motivations that are at play. The issue books spell out the consequences of each policy option for what citizens consider most valuable. Participants in the forums do the difficult work of deliberation—of moving toward a choice on each issue by weighing carefully the pros and cons of every option. The premise is that the pulls and tugs of having to make choices together will cause people to learn more about policy issues and move from individual opinions toward more shared and reflective judgments. The objectives of the forums are to help people become a public, to develop the skills needed for public politics, to speak in a public voice, and to contribute to defining the public's interests.

What began as a small group of institutions using the NIF approach has expanded each year so that now, throughout the country, thousands of organizations have made National Issues Forums a part of their own programs. They include colleges, universities, and secondary schools; libraries and leagues; churches, synagogues, and theological centers; literacy programs and leadership programs; and student associations and senior citizen centers. The NIF methods of analysis and discussion are also being adapted by citizens' organizations in other countries. After all, public deliberation is not an invention of the United States.

Things That Only the Public Can Do

We have a historical memory of town meetings in New England and of leaders of the public who were sometimes government officials (people such as John Adams). Many of us have been to, seen, or heard about a modern-day forum, even if it were no more than the highly informal "forum" of a coffee-shop discussion. So the public exists. Unfortunately, the public isn't necessarily connected to the government. Public talk and public assemblies are fine, but the conventional wisdom in the United States says that they aren't essential. Our political culture today doesn't reflect Jefferson's keen sense of the importance of "the voice of the whole people" and the "common reason of society." Some of us are not even sure there are such things. We don't have ready answers for the questions of what does the public contribute and what does it bring to the table. We have trouble making the connection between what happens in the forums we attend and what happens in the chambers of government.

Although the tie between the public and government is hard to define these days, it is there, and it is critically important. There are certain things that even the best governments and all of their experts can never do. There are certain things that only the public can do. Democratic governments cannot create their own legitimacy. They cannot define their own purposes or set the standards by which they will operate or chart the basic directions they are to follow. Although we often expect them to, governments cannot make and sustain tough decisions on issues that the country is unwilling to make or support. Democratic governments need broad public support if they are to act consistently over the long term. Their foundations are in the common ground for action that only the public can create. Governments can build common highways for us, but not common ground. And governments—even the most powerful—cannot provide the popular will needed for effective political action. Governments can command obedience, but they cannot create will. Finally, it is up to the public to transform private individuals into public citizens, people who are political actors. Citizens can create governments, but governments can't create citizens. Only citizens can do that.

Governments, national and local, in order to be legitimate in the eyes of the people, must act out of a sense of common public interest. But governments cannot serve the public's interests unless those interests are defined. No matter how good they are as guardians, the officials of government cannot be the sole judge of what those interests are. In a democracy, a NO SMOKING sign in public really means "we have decided there should be no smoking here." It means "No Smoking" is in the public interest. Absent our decision—and the support that must follow—signs, rules, and laws have little enduring effect.

The responsibilities for defining the public interest, describing the purposes and directions consistent with those interests, creating common ground for action, generating political will, and creating citizens are undelegable. They remain responsibilities of the public. Elliot Richardson, whose career has been in government, once said, "Although we, the people, have delegated limited responsibilities to those who hold public office in the interest of all of us, we, nevertheless, retain ultimate responsibility. We cannot delegate it; it belongs to us. We may fulfill it well or poorly, but still we have it."[22]

There is, in the broadest sense, political work to be done before the politics of governing—electing officials, passing laws—can be effective. We can elect our representatives but not our purposes. Political work is done in stages, with each stage doing the preliminary work that makes the next possible. Public choices about purposes are the necessary precondition for the governmental solutions we demand. The work that the public does begins in the primary stages—at the foundation—of politics. Even today, with elaborate systems of government and powerful groups organized as advocates on all kinds of issues, the public has the same essential work to do.

What Makes the People a Public?

If the public is indispensable to our politics, why don't officials find a public or a public voice more often? To argue that the public is missing from the political system is to say more than that individuals aren't being listened to or that people have been pushed out by experts and professionals. People have to become a public in order to sustain a democracy—in order to do those things that only a public can do. What, then, makes a public something more than a mass of people or an aggregate of interest groups?

If the question of what turns a collection of people into a public could be answered in just one word, the word would be *deliberation*. People become a public through the connecting process of deliberation. To deliberate is not just to "talk about" problems. To deliberate means to weigh carefully both the consequences of various options for action and the views of others. Deliberation is what we require of juries. It is what makes twelve of our peers a group to whom we literally give life-and-death powers. We don't just trust twelve people with those powers under any condition. We only trust them under the condition that they deliberate long and carefully. The same is true of democratic politics.[23] Without the discipline of serious deliberation, it is impossible for a body of people to articulate what they believe to be in the best interest of all—in the "public" interest. Deliberations are needed to find our broader and common concerns.

Public forums and public dialogue are responsible for the deliberation. The quality of those deliberations ultimately determines the quality of the actions that a representative government takes.

Without deliberation, people are just people, a collection of individuals, inhabitants, not a public. They have no connection or relationship to one another. Without becoming public citizens capable of giving common direction to government, people are capable of being little more than consumers of government services. And without deliberation, governments are left without public direction and legitimacy. Referendums become no more than collective knee jerks. Whether representative or direct, local or national, democracies require public deliberation. Deliberative politics is not the ideal politics; it is the necessary politics of a democracy.

Deliberation is not a rare human activity. People deliberate any time they are confronted with a serious question (to marry or not, to choose one particular career or not) and aren't sure of the answer. But we don't always bring deliberation into politics. We say all kinds of things when we talk politically. We proclaim and complain and exclaim. Most of all, we express. We speak as individuals about what we want, or don't like, or wish others would do. That is all well and good, but if that is all there is in our political conversations, we are in trouble.

Ralph Ketcham, an American historian, distinguishes between expressive and deliberative (what he calls "interactive") democracy in his work *Individualism and Public Life*. The assumption behind expressive democracy, Ketcham explains, is that society is a diverse aggregate of interests and of factions expressing those interests. Expressive democracy emphasizes giving people a chance to speak out or vote. Deliberative democracy, on the other hand, emphasizes the quality of public interactions and the opportunities to talk and think together.

Deliberative democracy also presumes that the purpose of political life is not to satisfy individual ambition but to create a good life in the community. In other words, "A true democratic polity involves a deliberative process, participation with other citizens, a sense of moral responsibility for one's society and the enhancement of individual possibilities through action in, and for, the *res publica*."[24]

This kind of democracy is not limited to governing by a process that allows a majority to rule over a minority. It is not a set of procedures. It is, in the philosopher John Dewey's words, a way of living. It is a way of living to maintain a good life in concert with others. This way of life, however, is possible only if people see themselves as public citizens.

The Deliberative Tradition in America

In 1919, a journalist, Glenn Frank, upon returning to the village where he was born, wrote an account of the deliberative tradition in American politics:

> To this day, when I return to this midwestern village and go to the post office, I am struck by the original and independent, although badly informed, thinking that is manifested in these free-for-all discussions. These men may wear "hand-me-down" or ready-made suits, but not so their opinions; they, at least, are personally tailored. They do not surrender their day's opinion to the chance impression of headlines. Each for himself as he goes about his work, they mull over such headline and hearsay information as may have come to them respecting the things that are holding the center of the stage in war, in diplomacy, in politics, and in industry; then later at the post office they lay their minds alongside the minds of their neighbors, they pit their opinions against the opinions of their fellows, and before they get through, they have made up the public opinion of the village.[25]

Although not as common as it needs to be, there is evidence of a deliberative tradition in America and its effect on public policies. Some of the evidence comes from a study of public attitudes over a long period, a half century. Individual attitudes can change precipitously over a short period, giving rise to the conventional belief that the public is uninformed and easily swayed by emotions, even to the point of favoring policies that do not correspond to their true values. Collective policy preferences, however, are a different matter according to a study by Benjamin Page and Robert Shapiro.[26] Their analysis of responses to thousands of questions on a wide variety of policy issues over fifty years shows that the public's attitudes are consistent, rational, and stable. Public preferences are stable in that they change incrementally in understandable responses to real changes in circumstances. Public attitudes are reasonable in that there are clear reasons for the attitudes; for example, people favor more spending on employment when unemployment is high. And the public's views are consistent in that the policies they favor do, over the long term, correspond to what people consider valuable.

Why are public policy preferences, over time and on the whole, so consistent, rational, and stable? Page and Shapiro conclude that it is because the "cool and deliberate sense of the community" eventually prevailed. Despite fewer post office conversations, enough of the deliberative tradition exists to have an effect. They warn, however, that political education, the process by which people educate themselves on policy issues, needs to be improved. They find that "the most conspicuous deficiency is the lack of opportunity for political learning through direct participation. In a country where only about half the eligible citizens vote in presidential elections, where town meetings are rare, where most workplaces are hierarchical, and where most citizens are not mobilized by a congenial issue-oriented party or political group, the educational potential of participation is not fully realized."[27]

Deliberation may occur, even under less than favorable circumstances, because Americans' culture nurtures what might be called an "instinct" for deliberation. College students, for example, who are usually taught politics as usual—and seldom deliberative democracy—will, nonetheless, describe the essential features of deliberative politics when asked about the kind of politics they would like to see practiced in the country.[28]

Unfortunately, most campuses seem to reinforce, perhaps unwittingly and certainly not alone, society's worst attitudes about politics. Students are particularly turned off by the tone of contemporary politics—by the extremes and negative tenor of what appears to be a grossly adversarial system with no regard for fair play. The debates that students hear, both on the campaign trail and in the classroom, appall them. A Wake Forest student complained, "People are very opinionated in my classes. There is no moderation at all and it [the discussion] gets totally out of bounds." Debates are dominated by extreme positions. People are punished for not being partisan zealots, so they drop out. On or off campus, political diatribes don't strike students as being capable of resolving the country's major problems. As one Morgan State student observed, "There are no solutions discussed; it is all rhetoric."

Although students may not normally spend much time thinking about politics, when pressed on the subject they say such things as, "There needs to be a better way." What they see happening in politics is quite different from what they would like to see. When given an opportunity, students seize the chance to imagine what politics might be like. They focus directly on the political dialogue. Although students would not like to see less emotion, they would like to see less acrimony. They wish there were more discussions where people listened as well as talked. They want to see more moderation, more appreciation for the indeterminate nature of political issues. They think that there should be more respect, more inclusion of different perspectives, not for the sake of being tolerant but for a very practical reason—to have a better understanding of the whole. Students want to know more about what the trade-offs are in the "solutions" they hear touted. They want to know how to make compromises with integrity and create common ground for action.

Obviously, students know what is missing in the political discussions they criticize—a diversity of perspectives, listening, and the careful weighing of trade-offs. They can even identify what they would need to practice a different kind of politics—the ability to keep an open mind, to stand in another person's shoes, to change, and to make decisions with others. These are, of course, the characteristics of deliberation, described amazingly well by young people who have little information on deliberative politics.[29]

In Glenn Frank's post office, the villagers did not take a survey to find out about public opinion. They did not depend on experts to make up their minds. They shaped the mind of the community through deliberation—through "pitting their opinions against the opinions of their fellows." These places for public discourse are indispensable. Today, there are a great many places for partisan talk.

That is not bad. But where are the places for deliberations on the interests of the public as a whole? Public institutions of all kinds—from civic associations, to leadership organizations, to libraries, to colleges and universities—have a special responsibility to provide for public deliberation. That responsibility is implied in their mandate for promoting public "education," an education that helps the public learn its business.

Notes

1. Arendt, *On Revolution*, 133.
2. Ibid., 118.
3. See Dorchester Antiquarian and Historical Society, *History of the Town of Dorchester*; Kuhns, *The "Mary and John"*; and Stark, *Dorchester Day*.
4. Arendt, *On Revolution*, 167; Elazar and Kincaid, "Covenant and Polity," 6.
5. See Brown, *Middle-Class Democracy*, ch. 5. Governor William Shirley of Massachusetts described town meeting participants as "mean" or common folk, and John Adams implied that voting in town meetings was not restricted by a tax qualification. Yet Brown also argues that other elections, like those in the province, were more democratic than has been assumed.
6. On the other hand, where town meetings were created as instruments of government authority, as they were in colonial Connecticut, they never played the role of purely public bodies. See Daniels, *The Connecticut Town*, ch. 3.
7. Zuckerman, *Peaceable Kingdoms*, 18–19.
8. Edwards and Richey, *The School in the American Social Order*, 83–84, as cited in Oliver, *The Art of Citizenship*, 7.
9. Merrill Jensen, ed., *Colonial Documents*, 280, as cited in Warden, "Boston Politics, 1692–1765."
10. See Brown, *Revolutionary Politics in Massachusetts*.
11. Webster, *The Works of Daniel Webster*, 1:135.
12. Arendt, *On Revolution*, 251.
13. Taylor, ed., *Massachusetts, Colony to Commonwealth*, ix–x.
14. Richardson, "We Delegated Our Powers," 2.
15. Arendt, *On Revolution*, 145.
16. Ibid., 145–46.
17. Jefferson, *Writings*, 1403.
18. Brown, *Middle-Class Democracy*, 78.

19. Oliver, *The Art of Citizenship*, 7–8.

20. See Overstreet and Overstreet, *Town Meeting Comes to Town*.

21. Ibid., 53.

22. Richardson, "We Delegated Our Powers," 3.

23. See Fishkin, *Democracy and Deliberation*. According to Fishkin, three conditions are necessary for a mature democracy: equity, nontyranny, and deliberation. Without deliberation to shape choices, the public's decisions are prone to be ignorant and unreflective and so lose their political authority.

24. Elshtain, "Democracy and the QUBE Tube," 108.

25. Frank, "The Parliament of The People," 402.

26. Page and Shapiro, *The Rational Public*, 384–85.

27. Ibid., 392.

28. The Harwood Group, *College Students Talk Politics*, vii.

29. Ibid., vii.

Part 4

Politics by Another Name

Never doubt that a small group of thoughtful, committed citizens can change the world; indeed it is the only thing that ever has.

—Margaret Mead

7

Politics That Is Not Called Politics

When citizens find themselves pushed out of "politics as usual," they often take matters into their own hands or, better said, turn to what they can get their hands on. They practice citizen politics. In discussions around the country, the very people who denied taking part in politics told stories about their own public participation.[1] A man from Des Moines described helping organize a neighborhood watch program; another from Dallas talked about being active in his local block association. Someone else from Des Moines reported, "I've been involved in schools—on parent advisory boards." A woman from Seattle said that people there were "working on getting the city to preserve open space." The person sitting next to her in the focus group pointed to citizens who were "organizing to take care of public parks." People described what they did to help agencies for low-income children, environmental groups, community-improvement coalitions, and various other civic associations.[2]

When they see the possibility of working with others to solve problems that concern them, many Americans—including those who disdain formal politics—volunteer for a variety of public activities and community problem-solving efforts. Although voting declined for decades, volunteering, including civic volunteering, appears to have increased. How much of the volunteering consists of individual acts of an altruistic sort and how much is political is not clear, although certainly much social action has a decidedly political dimension. Citizens, however, will not call what they do in these public activities "politics." Yet, if passing legislation on crime and water quality are political, it is hard to say that citizens organizing, not just to deal with symptoms but also to rid their communities of crime on the streets or pollutants in the drinking water, is not political.

Americans absolutely refuse to call these activities political because the word *politics* is so associated with what politicians and governments do. But citizen politics is very much politics. The word *politics* is rooted in the word *polis*, which the ancient Greeks used for city. Athens, for example, was a polis. Politics has to do with those activities in a polis needed to ensure a good common life. It is quite all right to think of politics as including a wide range of formal and informal efforts to solve common problems and advance the common well-being. Politics is acting publicly to foster the well-being of a polity. A neighborhood association trying to revitalize its community is political. A citizen coalition working for a better environment is political. A school board deciding on a budget is political. And all those interested in such efforts—in the character of the country or community where they live—have political interests. Politics is a natural activity for all humans. Government is one aspect of politics, but it is far from all of politics. Politics is not just for politicians. As Aristotle observed, "We are all political creatures by nature." Politics began in discussions in Athenian markets and popular assemblies long before there was an apparatus for government. John Maverick practiced politics in town meetings well before there was a mayor in Dorchester.

So there are actually two types of politics practiced in America: electoral (governmental) politics and citizen politics. The former is a politics dominated by politicians, lobbyists, and bureaucracies. The latter is the politics that people refuse to call politics. We see the first kind of politics in campaigns, ballot boxes, and speeches by the mayor. We find the second in neighborhood associations, public forums, and organizations for civic action.

Neither kind of politics can substitute or compensate for the other. The efforts of people turning to an informal type of politics do not offset the dangerous forces that drive people away from voting booths and make them utterly cynical about those who serve in government. Neither is one kind of politics the moral antithesis of the other. The politics of politicians and governments is not "bad" politics, even though many people cannot find a place in it. And citizen politics is not the "good" kind of politics, although many people find it "user friendly." Both types of politics are subject to corruption and produce their own forms of frustration.

When Americans practice the politics of everyday life, they organize publicly and act together to keep drugs out of the schools, safeguard the air they breathe, and help young people get a good education. Still, it is no wonder that most people don't think of this kind of activity as political or even as part of citizenship. If politics is about politicians and governments, then citizenship is, by this logic, limited to voting and obeying laws. You have to have the mayor or some official involved in order for an activity to be "political." From this mind-set, what people do together to solve common problems could not possibly be politics. Yet it is.

In fact, many Americans believe citizens have "an obligation to participate in such politics—to help out and do things in the community."[3] Whether this is thought of as the regular duty of a citizen or the voluntary acts of "an extra good citizen" is not the point. These are activities beyond voting and obeying the laws; they are civic and political. The point is that many people are already involved in politics of a broader and more inclusive sort. Although not everything is political, there is a political dimension to much of what we do.

We may be able to learn a great deal from citizen politics about how to remedy the estrangement of Americans from the politics of government. The standard and well-meaning strategies for "bringing people into politics" may be going at the problem backward. If people are already engaged in a kind of politics, the challenge is not to draw them out of their supposed apathy to become advocates in politics as usual. The challenge is to connect politics as usual to the politics that people already practice. Despite its frustrations, people find citizen politics natural, the sort of thing in which everyone can participate. Moreover, the politics that people won't call politics is a valuable resource. For instance, it provides most of the occasions when people can learn what it really means to be a citizen—and not just a consumer of services or a critic who holds officials accountable (more on this subject in the final chapter). Perhaps the political system should take on some of the qualities of citizen politics.

The Character of Citizen Politics

The conventional wisdom isn't aware of citizen politics because it is not found in the places we usually look for politics nor does it not have the character of what is conventionally understood as politics. The commitments citizens make in their public activities cannot be measured in the way we measure political commitment on election day. Also, we don't find citizen politics so much in city halls as we do in church basements, living rooms, and local restaurants. It occurs in what might be called "public spaces" because it is created by public citizens.

People sharply distinguish these public activities from politics because they don't have the feel of politics. Politics, citizens say, is dirty, messy, bureaucratic, and professional. It is the opposite of what they find in their civic activities. "Politics is rules, laws, policies," a woman from Los Angeles explained. "This has nothing to do with why I am involved in my community." Politics is seen as circumscribed and directed by someone else. People find little or nothing personal in it; there is no place for their initiative and action.

Public activities, on the other hand, allow for personal initiative and action. And they address what people describe as "the things that matter." Citizens believe that public problems can be acted on by people working together; political problems apparently cannot. One citizen said succinctly, "Community involvement brings about change—politics doesn't."

Some wish that politics as usual could be more like their civic work, saying, "It should be considered politics, but it's not." When comparing citizen politics to politics as usual, someone even went so far as to suggest that it "is political in a truer way. It's people organizing to make things better. That's what politics really is."

Is Citizen Politics Only Local Politics?

Because it is much easier to see citizen politics in community involvement, some dismiss it on the grounds that it is only applicable at the local level where people are dealing with friends and neighbors. Citizen politics is stereotyped as the kind of direct democracy that does not recognize the necessity of representative government. However, case studies of public problem-solving projects (chapter 8) challenge these misconceptions. The issues that people address locally can have both national and international implications; environmental protection is a case in point. Furthermore, citizens involved in public projects do not usually think direct democracy is the answer. They desperately want a more productive relationship with local and national governments. And they don't just work with people they know and like; they build alliances with people who are not necessarily like them.

The tasks of citizen problem solving in a community are much like the tasks citizens face in defining the public's interest nationally. To solve any problem, citizens first have to come to some shared understanding of the problem and a shared sense of what their interests and purposes are. Then they have to make some hard choices about the direction in which they want to move, about what, of all they consider valuable, will inform the actions they will take. Making these choices together and acting on them together requires the same kind of serious deliberation that deciding on national policy requires.

People turn to citizen politics and common problem solving not because it is more convenient, less controversial, and easier. They are driven to this kind of politics by forces that compel them to "organize to make things better."

The Driving Forces behind Citizen Politics

There are several of these forces. One is the desire for greater control over an uncertain future. Another is a drive to make things better by solving the problems that governments and politics as usual do not seem to solve—or may not be able to solve. Still another is a need to address deteriorating civic relationships and an absence of political cohesion (the ability to work together effectively).

Solving Problems to Gain Greater Control over the Future

Many Americans worry that their community (which could be a neighborhood, city, county, or state) is not as good as it could be and that its future is not as secure as they wish it were. They want it to be better.[4] Although people have different notions of what being better means, these differences don't dampen the quest; they spur it on. People talk—sometimes quite emotionally—about their desire to bring about change in their communities. When a man from Dallas was asked why he was involved in civic projects, he volunteered, as many others did, "I want to change things." People want to solve the problems that invade their lives and put their futures at risk.

A sense that the future is at risk provides a particularly powerful incentive to solve the problems at hand. Americans have personal as well as public experiences with losing control and being threatened by mounting problems. Personally, people feel they have less command over their own lives than they want. For example, fewer Americans believe that hard work will lead to success than was the case several years ago.[5] People in many cities also fear declining control over their futures. With the changing patterns of ownership in business, they worry that they are losing control of their economies to decision making in faraway boardrooms.

The Naugatuck Valley in western Connecticut is one of the areas where residents have felt an acute loss of economic control, a feeling that developed over time as plants were closed or sold. Residents worried that their economic future was being decided in cities far removed from the valley. As Reverend Tim Benson, president of the Naugatuck Valley Project, explained, "When somebody in London or Los Angeles owns a mill in the valley, you feel helpless and out of control."[6]

Other communities have had similar experiences as bank ownership has become more centralized and buyouts of local businesses have become common. Authors of a study of these economic trends report:

> Every wave of conglomeration and diversification seems to be followed in short order by a "shake-out"—the most dramatic symptoms of which are plant, store, and office closings. . . . Centralization is the aspect of modern capitalist development that gave rise to the process of conglomeration. But centralization has also undermined the economic stability of communities across the country indirectly, through its tendency to increase the degree of absentee control of a community's economic base. . . . The significance of this trend is that whether or not any particular "remotely controlled" business is actually reorganized or shut down by its absentee owners, the potential for this (or any other management decisions deleterious to the local economy) is greatly enhanced by the very fact of absentee control.[7]

Changes in economic control bring with them profound political shock. Bewilderment and resentment are common reactions. When a major oil company in Shreveport, Louisiana, was taken over by an out-of-state competitor, the managing editor of the local newspaper described the town's feelings: "There's a moment when you wake up and say, 'Damn, we don't own our own town anymore. When did this happen?'"[8]

Americans also want to get on with solving problems because some of the most serious ones seem to be increasing despite our best efforts to solve them. These are the problems that take advantage of a diminished sense of community and then further loosen the ties that bind people together. Crime is a prime example. According to criminologists, the signs of a community in decline (litter on the streets, loitering, public drunkenness, and broken windows in abandoned housing) create an environment in which more serious crimes, like robbery, drug dealing, and eventually murder, flourish.[9] As John Gardner has noted, this breakdown of communities is having a terrible effect on the behavior of individuals:

We have all observed the consequences in personal and social breakdown. The casualties stream through the juvenile courts and psychiatrists' offices and drug abuse clinics. There has been much talk of the breakup of the nuclear family as a support structure for children. We must remind ourselves that in an earlier era, support came not only from the nuclear family but from extended family and community. The child moved in an environment filled with people concerned for his future—not always concerned in a kindly spirit, but concerned. A great many children today live in environments where virtually no one pays attention unless they break the law.[10]

Crime and other community-related problems—and our inability to combat them—suggest that we are put at risk by social trends that are making the country "a random collection of atomized individuals . . . with no connectedness or responsibility for one another."[11] Social forces appear to be fragmenting society, threatening the work ethic, rendering the economy uncompetitive and people uncooperative and unable to deal with mounting social conflict and political polarization. These feelings are heightened by the perception that the nation is in competition with countries where people appear to work together more closely.[12] As Benjamin Barber put it, we worry that "beneath the corruptions associated with alcohol and drugs, complacency and indifference, discrimination and bigotry, and violence and fractiousness—is a sickness of community: its corruption, its rupturing, its fragmentation, its breakdown; finally, its vanishing and its absence."[13]

Building a Stronger Sense of Community

If there is no sense of community, it stands to reason that it will be difficult to solve common problems. A purely instrumental, problem-solving politics isn't adequate by itself. People in a community have to have public spirit and a sense of relationship. They have to be positively engaged, not just entangled with one another. Problems divide people, so if they do not create solid working relationships before difficulties mount, there is little likelihood that they can create any sense of community in the midst of major conflict.

The drive to belong, to be a part of a larger community, is one of the oldest and deepest of human drives.[14] In fact, being connected to others in families and political communities is part of what it means to be human. We see that impulse played out around us every day. Go to your local Chamber of Commerce directory and look at the number of organizations based on a sense of community—the civic clubs, fraternal associations, and religious organizations. People identify themselves by these attachments: "I am a Rotarian"; "I am a Baptist"; "I belong to the Garden Club." We identify with others by identifying with their community. "Ich bin ein Berliner" was President Kennedy's way of showing solidarity with the people of West Germany at the height of the crisis over the Berlin Wall.

Because "community" usually has positive connotations, people regret the loss of a sense of community in the country. Citizens lead fractious lives. They worry that people have become increasingly disconnected from one another and from the larger community. "We no longer have neighbors," lamented a woman from Richmond. "You say 'hello' but you don't really know them. We lost that togetherness to share and reach out." A man in Philadelphia gave reasons: "People move all the time. Six houses in a three-block area have been sold in the last month." When neighbors change regularly, people stop answering their doors after dark. They are fearful of, and take less interest in, one another.

This lack of community can be devastating politically. Effective community problem solving requires having places where citizens can come together and organize to act together. As one man observed, "The way to get influence is to get a gang of people together." Yet he concluded sadly, "We lack a sense of community. We're too busy to go out and develop a community, [and so] we will never get a gang together. We're in very big trouble." Scholars, in quite a different language, make the same point: Community attachment is essential to self-government because it engages citizens in "a common life beyond their private pursuits" and because it cultivates "the habit of attending to public things."[15]

Despite pervasive concerns about the loss of community, some citizens are finding success in "getting gangs of people together" to act on public issues. In fact, many of the same people who worry about a "loss of community" also testify to their own community involvement.

Community and Problem Solving

Is part of this longing for community a romantic fantasy about a harmonious, homogeneous existence, which can never exist in a pluralistic and competitive society? When people talk about the need for a stronger sense of community, do they mean they want to go back to a specific locale, a geographic community? Certainly there are those who do. The only way to make the country work, some argue, is through small community governments, so small that we can decide most issues by voting directly on them. History shows, say proponents of this kind of community, that small is beautiful.[16]

For others, "community" has a slightly different connotation. To be in a community means not to be alone and lonely but in contact with others. What people want is not necessarily harmony or the absence of differences but mutual respect and understanding. We like communal relationships because our dealings can be face-to-face and personal, not bureaucratized as they are in institutions.

Still others have negative reactions to "community." The community is the little town in which some grew up—and couldn't wait to leave. Or the community is the rather hypocritical force that intrudes on personal liberty. The community may refer to people who are all alike—and unlike me—and who behave accordingly. Community may connote the narrow and parochial. Some Americans are individualists in the mode of Daniel Boone; they want to be left alone to pursue their own interests. They are decent folk, but community is not all that important to them.

Certain senses of community are not very constructive in politics. Some communities get their sense of unity from opposing outsiders. Every day we read about communities that have found a new solidarity in fighting a proposed landfill or prison. This type of community action is protective action. In this sense, community is parochial, self-serving, and defensive.

The community that certain interest groups create can also be highly partisan, only concerned with what affects its members or advances their point of view. Community can mean me and mine banded together to protect ourselves from you and yours.

Most of us have probably experienced community both as something we wish to avoid and as something to join; we do not belong fully in either camp. That is, Americans are proudly individualistic, yet they like belonging to something larger than themselves—and not just to protect themselves from outsiders. Our most positive sense of community seems to call to mind particular ways of relating to one another and not just a particular town or geographic location. Often these are ways of solving problems together, so the location of "community" is in those places we go to address common problems.[17] These are typically associations of various kinds. And the relations we have there are more political than personal, so we are talking about political community.

Associations of citizens as citizens to solve common problems create a particular type of political community. They are not quite the same as Edmund Burke's "little platoons" of family and neighborhood. Nor are they the same as factions or special interest groups. They are made up of people with diverse points of view who have associated, for a time, to advance their common well-being. These associations have names like Confluence St. Louis, Mobile United, and First Mississippi. They exist within geographic and historical communities—in neighborhoods, cities, states, and in the country. In fact, our strongest cities and states seem to have networks of these associations—associations of associations. These networks create a circulatory system for citizen politics.

Why Do People Participate?

The central question is not, of course, what all the meanings of community are. The central question is, why do people associate in a citizen politics of public problem solving when they disdain and avoid the politics of government? The participants in citizen politics are quite clear about their reasons. They say, in effect,

"When I participate there will be at least the *possibility* to bring about and witness change." As reported in the second chapter, having a sense of possibility is no more than a feeling that there is an opportunity to make a difference.

The Power of Possibility

Possibility exists in citizen politics because people can be more than bystanders—more than observers of a political system. Citizens want to be engaged in politics personally. They want to address issues that really matter to them and hear what other people think about these issues. They want to rub shoulders with those people. They want to do more than write a letter, mail a check, or vote on election day.

A sense of possibility develops around issues that have meaning in people's everyday lives. Those are the issues people have a stake in addressing. Sometimes policy issues are clouded with technical or bureaucratic terms, so people have to translate these issues into their own terms in order to find how they affect what is valuable to them. If they are successful, they are more likely to become involved.

People see possibility, too, when they believe they can have a voice. Although Americans see little possibility of having a say in politics as usual, they often have just the opposite feeling about citizen politics. In the Harwood focus groups, many said they chose to become involved in community problem solving because what they had to say would be heard and valued.

People also see possibility in politics when they can actually get their hands into problem solving. They are not restricted to casting a vote, which they worry will have no effect, or to sending a letter, which they fear no one will take seriously. People can act directly; they can develop tutorial programs to help the schools; they can organize baseball teams for youngsters who need more adult attention; they can launch a program to recycle trash; and they can expand their individual influence by getting others to join with them in these civic projects.

When we get our hands on politics, it increases our sense of being in control. We all tend to believe that we can have an effect if we can just get at the problems that trouble us. What is more, getting our hands on a problem brings us closer to it so that we can, as one citizen put it, "see the effectiveness of [our work] while we're doing it." That intimacy feeds a sense that change is possible.

Politics with the Strength of Many

Finally, a sense of the possibility for change grows out of the banding together that occurs in citizen politics. Being associated with, and committed to, others gives people a feeling that they are equal to their problems. People who feel isolated feel hopeless. Citizen politics is an arena for common action, and people sense that common action is effective action. As one person put it, "I feel that one-on-one we are not going to have an effect." But, he added, "Collectively we can have a voice." Acting in cooperation with others energizes people. When asked why they become involved in a civic project, people say such things as: "I interact with people"; "I was doing it with someone else"; "You feel a part of things."

Comments like these demonstrate the connections between a sense of possibility, a sense of community, and the activity of problem solving. Solving problems together creates a sense of community—a sense of belonging—even if the people with whom we are working do not live in our neighborhood or even in the immediate area. We may not have a feeling of social unity, but we can have a sense of political solidarity. What often begins as a practical, problem-solving venture becomes a community-building enterprise.

Notes

1. The Harwood Group, *Citizens and Politics: A View from Main Street America*, 41–50.

2. According to a Gallup–Independent Sector survey completed in 1989, approximately 98.4 million Americans volunteer an average of four hours each week, an increase of 23 percent in numbers over three years. The Independent Sector identified eleven sites for volunteerism, including religious organizations, education groups, advocacy and public betterment groups, and political groups. See Quigley, ed., *Civitas*, 76–78.

3. Conover, Crewe, and Searing, "The Nature of Citizenship," 814–19.

4. Moore, *A Working Paper on Community*, 5.
5. Oreskes, "Alienation from Government Grows, Poll Finds."
6. Brecher and Costello, eds., *Building Bridges*, 94.
7. Bluestone and Harrison, *The Deindustrialization of America*, 160–61.
8. Gurwitt, "The Rule of the Absentocracy," 55.
9. Reppetto, "About Crime; with Order Comes Safety," 58.
10. Gardner, "Building Community," 73.
11. Leo, "Community and Personal Duty," 17.
12. Yankelovich, *New Rules*, 121–22.
13. Barber, "The Civic Mission of the University," 69.
14. Yankelovich, *New Rules*, 118–19.
15. Sandel, "Democrats and Community," 20.
16. See Bryan and McClaughry, *The Vermont Papers*.
17. McKnight, "Do No Harm," 8–9.

8

New Thinking

When the citizens quoted in the last chapter wished that politics as usual could be more like citizen politics, it was not an irresponsible fantasy. Citizen politics these days is filled with political "inventors," the equivalents of the Franklins, Edisons, and Wrights. They seem to thrive in problem-solving, community-building activities. This chapter is about the new or different thinking that informs what they do.

America's new generation of political inventors joins others throughout the world who are trying to find different ways to solve old problems. Citizens everywhere are throwing off old institutions, parties, and ideologies. Look at the former Soviet Union and at Eastern Europe and Latin America. Although without as much drama, the same kind of search for new ways goes on in Gould, Arkansas, Kalamazoo and Grand Rapids, Michigan, and Englewood, New Jersey. Of course, whether anything is really "new" in politics is questionable. But there are those who go beyond the conventional wisdom. They see politics differently, and they go about their work in novel ways.

What follows are examples illustrating the principles of this new thinking. These examples aren't necessarily success stories. But they do reveal striking departures from business as usual.

The Impetus for New Thinking

At some time or another, the tried-and-true methods don't work or don't seem applicable to the problems at hand. Often these are the kinds of problems mentioned earlier—the problems that grow out of and exacerbate a weak sense of community. In some cases, our goals change; we want to do more than adjust to a problem, we want to make systemic changes to get at the source of a problem. So we experiment with strategies that, if not new, are at least different. We want to add to the standard techniques for solving problems.

Of course, much can go wrong. New directions fail to attract popular support. Even friends and neighbors may oppose change. "Gatekeepers," unelected power brokers, can block initiatives by withholding their approval, which makes others reluctant to act. Balkanization, historic rifts in the body politic, makes new levels of cooperation difficult. The list of obstacles goes on. Even the best of the new approaches to politics can run aground.

Still, those who begin to work together in different ways sometimes find that they begin to think about politics in fresh and creative ways. These people, their methods, and—most of all—their ideas deserve our attention because they add significantly to the conventional wisdom. It is difficult, however, to know what to call their efforts. *New, inventive,* or *creative* are self-serving terms. They imply that the conventional wisdom is always wrong—but it isn't. Because much of what is being attempted in the "new" strategies is community-based and involves putting the community itself—the public—in the center of politics, the term *community* or *citizen politics* would be a fit term for what adds to conventional politics. These two kinds of politics have different assumptions, tactics, and, in some cases, goals.

Conventional politics concentrates more on getting to solutions quickly; citizen politics concentrates on carefully defining and, if need be, redefining problems before moving to solutions. Conventional politics stresses the need for leaders who will create "solutions." Citizen politics stresses the importance of citizens claiming their own responsibility and becoming solutions themselves. Conventional politics emphasizes using existing power wisely and empowering the powerless. Citizen politics emphasizes creating new forms of power at all levels of a community. Conventional politics' resources are more financial and legislative; citizen politics uses public will as its primary political capital. Conventional politics assesses people's needs; citizen politics assesses their capacities. While conventional politics uses a language of advocacy and "winning," citizen politics uses a language of practical problem solving and relationship building. Conventional politics is more about having diversity; citizen politics is more about using diversity and getting diverse groups to work together. Conventional politics looks on the public as a source of accountability; citizen politics looks to the public for direction. Conventional politics gives citizens information; citizen politics teaches the skills of effective public action. Conventional politics is about coordinated action; citizen politics is about complementary or collaborative action. Conventional politics creates public events; citizen politics creates public space.

The Principles

In most communities, there was a time when a small elite could decide what problems were to be solved and how. There were tried-and-true formulas for solving problems. Usually, a small group of leaders could marshal the needed resources, which were primarily financial, to build a new civic center or museum or assemble enough volunteers to cope with a natural disaster. Although that practice has its advantages, it no longer seems to work in many communities. So different operating principles emerged.

On Responsibility

There are communities stuck in bemoaning the ills that have befallen them. Others have moved on to recognize that they have to act themselves; they can't wait on outside forces to save them. Citizen politics begins when citizens take responsibility for their fate, when they "own" their problems.

Claiming the Future When the plants closed in the Naugatuck Valley, Theresa Francis, who chaired the local UAW's steering committee, wrote the first principle of new thinking: "All workers have to realize that we're responsible for our own condition. If we don't devote some time to our unions, our political party, our church organization, and the laws being enacted, we'll wake up and find ourselves with empty pension funds, bankrupt companies, disproportionate sacrifices and a run-down community."[1]

To emphasize the importance of claiming responsibility, Harry Boyte, who studies what is happening in community action around the country, uses the story of Bertha Gilkey, the leader of a tenants' project in St. Louis. Bertha Gilkey lives in a public housing project, Cochran Gardens, which today is noted for flower-lined paths, clean buildings, play equipment, and social cohesion. She lived in this very same housing project when it was filled with "drugs, crime, prostitution, garbage and urine in the halls, broken windows, graffiti."[2] While the Gardens may not be perfect, the changes were dramatic and profound.

Improvements began with a simple but powerful first step. Evidently, one of the major problems in the project was vandalism of the laundry room. When the machines were destroyed, the tenants demanded that the project's management install new ones. Even when pressured by rent strikes, the management was increasingly resistant to throwing good money after bad.

One day the tenants added a new tactic to their strategy, which set in motion a transformation of the Gardens. The first goal for Bertha Gilkey and her neighbors was a locked and painted door for the laundry. The tenants raised funds in the project to buy a lock and a few cans of paint. It wasn't much, but it demonstrated that the tenants could do something on their own. Next came a campaign to get everyone to paint their hallways. Then, the tenants approached the building management. This time they had more than needs and demands; they had capacities and even accomplishments. They had something to offer. In time, the often-troubled tenant-management relationship changed for the better. As the tenants took responsibility for themselves, they ceased to be wards of the manager. Tenants became the planners rather than the "planned for." They became citizens of their neighborhood, not just inhabitants of a housing project. The Gardens, although still beset with all the challenges of a low-income housing project, began to live up to its name.[3]

Becoming the Solution By claiming responsibility, people develop a sense that "they are the solution" rather than bystanders or victims. They believe they can make a difference. Citizen organizations that begin by searching for the one "correct" answer to a problem often come to realize that there really isn't any one solution. They realize that they themselves, with their commitment and energy, are a large part of the answer to what ails their community. As two founders of a clean water project along the Tennessee River put the principle, "People have to provide their own hope. Nobody's going to come along and make everything all better. It's us. We're the problem, we're the solution."[4]

The citizens who participated in the Tennessee River project no longer saw themselves as victims, they saw themselves as "agents." They believed they could do something. Why? They saw that they understood the problem at hand as well as any experts because they had experienced it personally. And they knew they were there to stay. Solutions would come and go. They wouldn't. Although funding for their project might end, they weren't going to leave.

This new thinking is not confined to the Tennessee River case. Other citizens' organizations have hit upon these same ideas, organizing around the principle of "becoming actors rather than casualties"[5] and seeing an active citizenry as the "permanent solution."[6]

Starting Inside, Moving Out The change in Cochran Gardens follows a pattern found in other community action projects.[7] Change begins within. First, people claim their own responsibility and concentrate on what they can do for themselves. Later, they draw in outside support. "Starting within" strategies are not the same as pull-yourself-up-by-your-own-bootstraps strategies. Bootstrap strategies ignore the principle of interdependence, that no one group has all the resources to achieve its objectives. The idea is not that everyone has to go it alone, but that the direction of change has to move from inside to outside. As the *Handbook of the East Los Angeles Community Union* says emphatically, "We see community economic development as a process by which communities take the lead from within, and attempt to realize their full human resource potential and improve their quality of life."[8]

On Capacity

Starting inside is possible when communities appreciate their innate capacities. Efforts to make social service systems more effective, coupled with experiments in community organizing, have produced some new thinking about people's capacity to act on their sense of responsibility. These new thinkers are civil rights advocates and community organizers who were, and continue to be, admirers of the late Saul Alinsky, a central figure in community organizing most known for his work in Chicago. They are trying to adapt his ideas to different situations.

Emphasizing What People Have No one who lives in a community impoverished by a weak economy, or who sees people ill, homeless, and burdened by problems that are not of their own making, is unaware that people have needs. It is only natural that much of problem solving is based on meeting those needs. One of the standard tools in conventional politics is "needs assessment."

Emphasizing needs, however, tends to have unintended and unfortunate political side effects. People lose a sense of their capacities. One urban philosopher and community organizer, John McKnight, has created "capacity" surveys in order for citizens to recognize their personal capacities and in order for communities to identify their untapped resources.

Creating viable economies in low-income areas is one of the major objectives of capacity surveys. Any skill or craft that has economic potential is prized. Low-income areas are not treated as pits of consumption but rather as sources of production. For example, one Chicago neighborhood organization interviewed residents of a low-income area to identify any experiences that had developed marketable skills. Among those interviewed—mostly women—the most common work experience was in health care. After identifying fifty people who felt they had a capacity to work in this field, the organization placed an advertisement in the local paper that said "Health Care Workers Available." Within one week, every one of the fifty was employed within eight blocks of where they lived.[9]

The post-Alinsky strategy is to build communities through restoring local economies, thus combining politics (community building) with economic development. The connection is essential, McKnight argues, because it makes no sense to practice politics as if economics did not exist, or economics as if politics did not exist.[10] This combined strategy treats people's political ability—their ability to organize themselves effectively—as a key economic capacity.

The idea of capacity, as contrasted with needs, is also central to McKnight's proposal for reforming the social service system. He argues that by seeing people primarily in terms of their needs, the social service system misses the potential in people's capacities. Every person can be seen as a glass half empty or half full, McKnight argues. By labeling people with the names of their deficiencies, professionals miss what is most important to people—opportunities to "express and share their gifts, skills, capacities, and abilities."[11]

These perspectives have led McKnight and others to conclude that community-based associations have to be built on recognizing the full potential of each citizen because the sum of everyone's capacities represents the power of the group. "Communities," he writes, "depend on capacities."[12]

On Power

No concept of politics can fail to deal with power and its uses. Citizen politics respects the reality of power while not accepting the standard definitions. Power is usually defined as control over existing resources. Power is money, legal authority, and control over institutions. That sort of power flows one way—from those in power to those who are powerless. Power is something used on people; it is coercive.

When power is defined as control over scarce resources, power transactions are necessarily a zero-sum game. Citizen politics argues that there are many kinds of political power, that power always flows in more than one direction, and that even those who have no formal power have other types of power to bring to bear on "the powerful." Certain citizens' groups are finding that power can be an expanding resource. Power, by their lights, has to be created and recreated—and it can be. From this perspective, the only true power is the power people create themselves. Power that is given by someone to empower others is not real power.

Creating Power Larry Susskind, who has studied ad hoc citizen groups, found that these groups have a variety of types of power at their disposal: the power of a good idea, the power of information derived from their experience, the power of their commitment (the willingness to act on what they say), and the power that grows out of relationships they have formed. Perhaps Susskind would be willing to add McKnight's definition of power to his list—the power of a group's aggregate capacities. No one would deny the reality or force of formal power; the point is only that power comes in many forms.[13]

These alternate sources of power differ from formal kinds of power because they are not zero-sum powers. They can all expand or grow without anyone losing power. In fact, these more public types of power tend to increase as they are used. One idea can generate another, one commitment can inspire another, one relationship can lead to another.

Moving from Moralized Power to Pragmatic Power The type of citizen-generated power that is most commonly recognized is moral power, the force of citizens' insistence that a law or custom is wrong. Almost everyone would understand Norman Cousins's testimony to the importance of this moral power: "Governments are not built to perceive great truths. Only people can perceive great truths. Governments specialize in small and intermediate truths. They have to be instructed by their people in great truths."[14]

The moral power of citizens has been a significant force in American politics from the civil rights movement to protests over the Vietnam War. Still, it may be a mistake to let these vivid examples create the sense that citizens' power is exclusively moral. Sometimes moralizing can be ineffective—when no one listens or when the moralizing is intolerant, excessive. So citizen politics focuses attention on the power that comes from the practical ability to work together and solve problems. Recognizing the difference in these two kinds of power has been very instructive. Perhaps it was the limitations of moralized power that caused a community organizer in Baltimore to report that his group learned they could be right all they wanted to, but it didn't make any difference.[15]

In many instances, citizens' power has come from the practical ability to work with others to solve a problem. The *Dayton Daily News* did a series on such projects, which it described as "alternative democracy." The series included reports on a tribe of Indians meeting in tiny Arctic villages to protect caribou; three hundred local citizens joining forces in an Ohio county to eliminate a source of air pollution; six thousand people organizing to preserve a historic farm in North Carolina; and six people sitting around a kitchen table in a low-income neighborhood in Washington, D.C., making plans to stop drug traffic on their streets. The newspaper did not seem to have any problem finding stories.[16] Although everyone interviewed thought what they were doing was moral or right, the projects were based on practical, get-the-job-done tactics.

Power Over; Power With New thinking or, better, different thinking about power goes back to the work of an early twentieth-century organization theorist, Mary Parker Follett. She argued that power can be either one-directional "power over" or interactive "power with." Starting with the conviction that true power is rooted in our individual capacities, Follett argued that genuine power could not be delegated or transferred. She thought sharing or giving power away was impractical and unrealistic. Power has to be grown, and it grows out of people's experience, knowledge, character, and, in politics, out of their associations or ways of relating.[17]

Joining individual capacities produces "power-with," or relational power. Two or more individuals joining forces to push a car off the road is a simple illustration. Relational power is the type of power people used in Cochran Gardens. The tenants had little authority, but they knew that authority was not the same as power. The tenants created power—first by combining their own individual capacities, and second by changing their relationship to the building's manager. Both tactics illustrate "power with." People can create relational power by deliberately changing the way they relate.

On Relationships

As these ideas about power demonstrate, much of the new thinking in politics grows out of a sense of how important relationships are in politics. So many fundamental problems have proven to be problems of relationships that some citizen organizations have concluded that fundamental change can be made only by fundamentally changing the working relationships in the community— the ways people habitually deal with one another. The idea is not to have "good" relationships in the usual sense of familiar and happy associations. The idea is to construct relationships conducive to problem solving, even when people aren't happy with, or don't necessarily like, one another.

This insight about the importance of relationships in politics is similar to insights about relationships in business. Businesses that aren't doing well often will change the way they do business; they will restructure working relationships. Changing relationships in politics means making changes in two ways of interacting—among citizens and between citizens and governments.

Restructuring the Citizen-Government Relationship Citizens don't usually see their organizations as substitutes for governments. They often want governments to work with them, not just for them. They want a different relationship with the agencies of government. To get officials to work with them, citizens are changing the way they relate to officeholders.

In *Governing* magazine, Jeffrey Katz wrote about the accomplishments of citizen-based organizations in addressing the problems of housing and business space for people with low incomes. Using figures from the National Congress for Community Economic Development, Katz reported that community groups built nearly 125,000 houses and developed 16.4 million square feet of space for retail buildings, offices, and industries. He found that citizens' organizations had used new tactics to get these results. "In making this transformation," he wrote, "neighborhood activists find that they spend less time pleading with government at any level for grants and subsidies. They spend a great deal of time trying to persuade governments to join with them." As Robert Zdenek, president of a Chicago neighborhood association put it, "If you're doing advocacy, it's more confrontational, more strident. If you're doing development, it's more collaborative."[18] These more collaborative relationships are based on pragmatic considerations—on doing what it takes to solve a problem.

Shifting from Identifying "the Enemy" to Building Pragmatic Ties Some grass-roots organizations that had specialized in fighting city hall have become much more pragmatic, moving away from strategies based on identifying the "enemies of the people" and trying to make them meet citizens' needs.[19] These community-based organizations are now teaching citizens how to build functional relationships with city hall. These relationships are based on respecting the interests of the other party. Harry Boyte uses the following example to describe such relationship building: "When leaders of Baltimore BUILD, the nation's largest mainly black local organization, first met with Senator Paul Sarbanes, he smiled, took out his notebook and asked, 'What can I do for you?' 'Nothing,' replied the leaders. 'We're here to get to know you. We want to know why you're in the U.S. Senate, what are your interests and concerns. We think that will help us develop a working relationship over time.'"[20]

This illustration does not mean that citizens' groups no longer find any officials or policies that are unjust and oppressive. It just means that certain groups have learned that it is better not to start with that assumption. It is useful to establish a constructive relationship as a basis for dealing with unintended aggravations.

Joining Diverse Groups of Citizens in "Public Relationships" The idea of functional or public relationships is at the heart of alternative ways of joining together diverse groups of citizens, citizens that don't necessarily have the same ideological orientation or identical interests. Citizen groups are finding new ways to build pragmatic relationships among the various elements of a community, even when there are legitimate differences among them.

The Naugatuck Valley Project mentioned earlier was led by a citizens' group that brought diverse interests into such a public relationship. It was a regional coalition of more than fifty religious, community, labor, and small business organizations. Diversity was important because the more diversity in such groups, the more talents and strengths there were to draw on. The emphasis was on "banding together," which the people involved saw as an accomplishment in itself. As Theresa Francis from the Naugatuck project explained the principle, "If all the people in the city are banded together to make it a better place to live, then it will be a better place to live. That's what Naugatuck Valley Project is all about."[21]

This emphasis on finding ways for diverse groups to work together stands in some contrast to the more conventional emphasis on having diversity. In a *U.S. News & World Report* story on New York, Mayor David Dinkins was quoted as referring to the city's racial and ethnic groups as a "gorgeous mosaic." But another New Yorker, Felix Rohatyn, was quick to remind the mayor that a mosaic needed glue to hold the pieces together.[22]

New thinking concentrates on bringing together all the parts of a community, in all of their differences. Creating a majority is not enough. No one today has made this point better than Mary Parker Follett: "Our rate of progress . . . depend[s] upon our understanding that man . . . gets . . . power through his capacity to join with others to form a real whole, a living group."[23] "Give *your* difference, welcome *my* difference, unify *all* difference in the larger whole— such is the law of growth."[24]

On Political Will and Interests

From the perspective of citizen politics, the most essential resource in a community is public will—the willingness or commitment of citizens to work on a problem until they have it under control. Will is essential in attacking those systemic "we-can't-seem-to-get-rid-of-them" problems that grow out of a lack of community and then further destroy community. Described as "more than dollars," political will is seen as the most important kind of political capital.

Seeing Connections Public will is conventionally thought of as a massive outpouring of civic duty born of an enlightened commitment to the common good. Citizen politics, however, tends to be more pragmatic, and its formula for building public will is based on working with existing interests rather than trying to replace them with one "general will." The idea is not to rely on a "guiding hand" that will serve the interest of all through the competition of selfish interests. The idea is to join existing interests, and the energy associated with them, in order to create a larger public will. This way of thinking about generating will is quite compatible with the new thinking about building functional political relationships. In both cases, the strategy is to get people to see the connections among their interests to produce "combined energy."[25]

Public will has certain qualities. It is the will of the many, certainly not everyone, but enough people to get the job done. It is more than the perseverance of a few. It certainly means more than fanatical devotion to one cause. Will connotes staying power or determination, not just initial popular support. Usually people have to be willing to make sacrifices. Public will goes deep into a body politic; it is not a superficial enthusiasm. The most dramatic illustrations of political will probably come from war—as seen in the determination of the people to protect their homeland against overwhelming military forces. Making connections, seeing relationships, appreciating the ties between what is valuable to me and what is valuable to you—these are essential to creating public will.

Making connections as a strategy for generating public will worked for the owners of floating homes on Lake Union near Seattle, Washington. It helped them keep both their homes and the lake. Proposed development plans for the lake area would have forced homeowners out of the floating homes they had occupied for years. The key to the success of the Floating Homes Association, according to one of its members, was that its members built support around the notion that the lake was a common good, a "gift from the Ice Age to the people of Seattle," rather than arguing just for the interests of the floating homes. As a result, small businesses around the lake joined in the effort, as did environmental groups. Sacrifices had to be made: homeowners, for example, had to agree to pay for sewage lines to keep from polluting the lake. The work to protect the lake and its inhabitants took years of effort. Yet, it has not only continued, but it has also spread its influence to the entire city over two decades.[26]

To summarize, communities can create public will by linking together inclinations, motivations, and interests that already exist, rather than attempting to create some new super WILL. The way we get energy from batteries is a rough analogy. Their power varies according to the way batteries are joined. Put a hundred 1.5 volt batteries separately in a row, link their tops together by one wire and their bases by another, and the energy produced is still 1.5 volts. Connect the batteries—actually join them end to base so that positive poles touch the opposite negative poles—and the result is quite a shock. Powerful public will seems to be created in the same way, by connecting existing energies.

On Action

A major obstacle to generating public will, of course, is that people don't always make key connections. Well-intended efforts are fragmented into an ineffective jumble of unilateral responses. Conventional thinking tries to deal with fragmentation of effort through coordination and accountability. Disappointments with enforcing coordination and accountability, however, are prompting some new thinking.

Using the Public to Unify Fragmented Activities Fragmentation of effort begins in all too common "solution wars." We often hear people say that "everybody knows what the problem is." Actually, what everyone "knows" is usually just his or her own experience with the problem. Communities have been known to spend their energy debating which of a number of predetermined solutions is best, little aware that there is no agreement on the nature of the problem. For example, widening a road might be defined as a problem of access by a merchant who depends on a flow of traffic, or as a problem of intrusion by a homeowner who wants privacy. It is easy to see why solution wars lead to political polarization, with everyone divided into camps, each advocating one particular solution or another.[27] Even a shared definition of a problem does not guarantee a solution—interests will still differ. But we cannot even begin to agree on how we should act until we have a common definition of the problem, one that reflects an understanding of our own interests, the interests of others, and how the two diverge and converge.

Fragmentation continues in the way we organize to deal with problems. We typically attack a large problem by breaking monumental tasks into small projects and dividing the responsibility among various agencies. While the intention is better management, the result is often the loss of connections among various facets of a problem. Take the problem of young people growing up at risk. For youth at risk—pregnant teens, drug abusers, high school dropouts, and kids from broken homes—there are as many agencies providing services as there are labels for what afflicts them. Yet, despite the growing seriousness of the problems of young people, few, if any, cities or states have a policy that coordinates all the available governmental and nongovernmental services. Typically, young people are put into categories according to the particular difficulty that brings them to our attention. Then they are divided into groups served by various agencies. As a result, we have young dropouts being handled by school officials, teenaged mothers-to-be participating in a federal nutrition program, and children with emotional problems being treated by church counseling programs. Although each of those services is beneficial, the left hand does not necessarily know what the right is doing.

Finally, fragmentation can grow out of turf battles between agencies. For example, both the U.S. Department of Labor (under job training partnership legislation) and the Department of Health and Human Services (under family support legislation) allocate funds for employment and training because neither feels the other's program is really what is needed.[28] Both use different definitions to describe the populations they serve, even though community leaders say the two end up serving many of the same people.[29] This division in the federal effort is then magnified many times when state, county, and city governments enter the scene with their differing programs, regulations, and procedures.

Of all the quite visible problems our communities face, fragmentation is one of the most serious because it is the problem behind the problem. The real difficulty, says former Secretary of Health, Education and Welfare John Gardner, is that our communities are often unable to pull themselves together, to act as coherent entities. Various parts of a community can have sharply different purposes and little talent for understanding one another. Consequently, what is in the best interest of the public as a whole gets lost in tensions, cross purposes, and stalemates.[30]

Conventional politics tries to deal with fragmentation by holding each agency to stricter rules of accountability or by imposing coordination. Citizen politics is based on the proposition that the public is the only force capable of bringing all of the parties to the table and transforming competitive activity into complementary or collaborative action. For example, Newark, New Jersey, with a third of its families living below the poverty level in 1980, created the Newark Collaboration. Although opinions differ on who was responsible for Newark's revival by the end of the decade, most agree that one decisive factor was this communitywide collaboration and a public that had "learned to work together across racial, interest, sector, and economic boundaries."[31] Much the same thing happened in Lincoln, Nebraska, through the Star Venture project and a "bottom-up" rather than "top-down" consensus-building process. The most important result of the Lincoln project was not just the new direction set for the city but "the change in the way in which the citizens of Lincoln did business."[32]

Choice: The Inescapable First Step

New thinking in politics often uncovers old wisdom. The basic premise behind some of the strategies we hear about today is a precept William Jennings Bryan enunciated some time ago: "Destiny is not a matter of chance—it is a matter of choice." Communities are what they are because of the choices they have already made; they will be what they will be because of the choices they will make in the future.

In its most basic form, taking responsibility for our fate begins in recognizing that we have choices. Recognizing our power to choose does not imply that we aren't subject to external forces beyond our control. Choices come from the way we respond to those circumstances. Someone would be a "complete slave," Simone Weil, a philosopher, argued, if what he or she did were controlled by the bad things other people do. We are only really free if what we do is directed by our inner sense of what we think we should be, by our own choices.[33]

Of course, choices are not usually "given." No one says, "Here are your choices, make them as you will." People have to claim their right to make choices, just as they have to claim their responsibility for what happens to them.

Citizen Politics and Choice Work

There are two ways to understand the process of making choices. Conventionally, the public's choices are understood to be decisions about the various solutions that the political system generates. Politicians and governments propose options for economic recovery or health coverage or tax relief. These are usually very technical and involve complex pieces of legislation. The public isn't the source of such options; citizens are just expected to choose among those that politicians, governments, and interest groups offer—in much the same way that consumers choose merchandise off the shelf. These selections are presumed to be guided by self-interests.

Another way to think of choices is to treat them as more fundamental issues of purpose. The most basic choices citizens make are about what kind of community and country they want. These choices aren't the same as preferences for one solution or another. People really can't select a particular solution until they have made more fundamental choices about purposes. The primary political challenge, from this perspective, is to answer basic questions like, What do we want for our community? What do we want our community to be?[34]

Finding out what a community wants could degenerate into a long wish list or an ethereal vision. The question becomes practical, however, when put in the context of particular issues. Communities never decide what they want once and for all. They choose what they want to be when they decide what to do about taxes and education and services—issue by issue. No community can become what it hopes to be without someone making some tough decisions. Certainly, individuals understand that no one can realize personal ambitions without making difficult decisions. Why should a community be any different? As basic and obvious as that principle is, it is often overlooked in the rush to find solutions or, alternatively, to create a vision of the perfect community. In neither case is the public asked to make any tough decisions. Making choices is left out of the political equation. In many communities, citizens haven't even understood and framed problems so that the public knows what issues it faces. Yet making choices about "what we want and what we should do" is the indispensable beginning to defining shared purposes, creating enough common ground for action, and generating political will.

The most basic choices citizens make do not turn so much on expert facts or legislative plans as they do on what is valuable to people. Basic choices force people to consult their deepest motives. Yet many things are valuable to us, and even if most of us can appreciate these "values," we still differ on which should guide us in making a choice on a particular policy issue. Setting policy direction is always difficult, especially when it comes to allocating the burden or pain that is inescapable in some situations. When people confront the costs and consequences of the options, they react with an anger and denial that is all too human. People are programmed to avoid painful decisions, collectively as well as individually. Making choices is hard work; citizens have to work through their initial reactions to the point that they are in control again and can deal with unpleasant realities.[35]

A great deal of new thinking has gone into getting communities into the habit of dealing with choices in such public terms—and into the habits of choice work. Citizens from Indianapolis, Indiana, conducted focus groups so they could frame local issues around choices reflective of what citizens considered valuable. The North American Association of Environmental Educators, a network of hundreds of people in nature centers, community colleges, secondary schools, and universities, is doing its issue books in a public choice format. A neighborhood association in Independence, Missouri, has, for a number of years, used the National Issues Forums books to develop new habits of analyzing and discussing issues. Syracuse, New York, is one of several cities that has conducted public choice campaigns. These campaigns have involved the media, as well as civic and educational organizations throughout the community, in facing up to the hard choices that have to be made on such issues as drugs and economic competitiveness. As a means of community building, citizens in Kalamazoo, Michigan, are working to establish choice-based forums that involve people from all sections of the city.[36]

Making public choices requires the kind of deliberation described in chapter 6. If communities don't deliberate, the choices they make are more likely to be relatively uninformed, knee-jerk reactions. The community will be guided more by mass opinions than by reflective and shared public judgments. On the other hand, when there is deliberation, people make surprisingly hard choices of the kind politicians sometimes avoid. That was the *Washington Post* columnist William Raspberry's conclusion after listening to citizen juries work their way through the federal deficit.[37]

Education for a Different Kind of Politics

Educating citizens for citizenship is central to new thinking. Traditional citizenship education focuses on giving people expert information, preparing them to evaluate critically what they are told, instructing them in voting practices, informing them on the structures of government, and inculcating a sense of duty. Traditional leadership programs also prepare a select few to be the "producers of solutions" that formal politics requires. The training concentrates on ways leaders can sell the public on their solutions and persuade people to vote for them.

Citizen politics argues for a very different sort of education. In citizen politics, citizens are the primary producers because they have to make the choices that give direction to governments and define the common purposes of community. Their education has to prepare them for making choices together, for creating power, for building relationships, and for generating political will. Leaders aren't so important as leadership, understood as a number of tasks that move a community from where it is to where it wants to be. From this perspective, a community needs leadership from every sector of the society, not just from a few people.[38] This sort of leadership is more than the exercise of authority. Leadership is marshaling the resources needed for change, not the management of institutional stability.[39] Citizens are responsible for this kind of leadership.

Educating people for civic leadership requires not so much teaching as learning by reflection on experience. But teachers are needed, teachers who can draw out and help name experiences rather than just instruct a passive audience. For example, to prepare people in low-income neighborhoods to be active citizens, Gerald Taylor, a community organizer in Tennessee, conducts a "school" that teaches political concepts rather than the traditional how-to's. His kind of community organizing puts a premium on building public relationships, so he teaches the concept of relationship. He does it by getting people to reflect on their own experiences with relationships, with the factors that make relationships either productive or not. Citizens then act on the concept in the way they go about banding together and dealing with city officials. Taylor's educational program is based on giving people ideas about how to practice politics differently. He doesn't hesitate to emphasize political theory, although he does it in a practical way. For him, theories are just ideas about practice.

Harry Boyte directs a similar political education program at the University of Minnesota's Humphrey Institute. This program works with teenagers and others to make politics their own by teaching them how to deal with the issues that they really care about. Teenagers have much the same feelings about politics that adults do. They believe it is foreign; they think about those sleazy politicians they see on television. Yet, teenagers have a positive reaction to the word *public*. It makes them think of public parks, public concerts, and people like themselves. So Boyte teaches the concept of "public politics." The teenagers in the program learn how they can use citizen politics to deal with problems that affect their everyday life—problems from crime and race relations to their relations to their schools—in public ways, by claiming responsibility, by creating their own power, and, as in Taylor's school, by building public relationships.

This public life project, while focused on problem solving, has many of the characteristics of Taylor's. Both teach theory as tied to practice. The ultimate objective of both programs is not to give people techniques but to enable them to change the character of politics. Conventional thinking in political education teaches politics as a series of transactions to be mastered. New thinking teaches concepts in order to enable people to transform politics.

Notes

1. Brecher and Costello, *Building Bridges*, 93.
2. Boyte, *Community Is Possible*, 98.
3. Ibid., 95–114.
4. Myczack, "We're the Solution," 19.
5. Fry-Winchester, "New Solution to an Old Problem," 9.
6. Cohen, "Tenants Bring Pride."
7. For example, see the case of the Kenilworth-Parkside development in northeast Washington in Osborne and Gaebler, *Reinventing Government*, 59–65.
8. National Commission on Neighborhoods, *People Building Neighborhoods*, 7.
9. Raspberry, "Cargo Cult."
10. McKnight and Kretzmann, "Community Organizing in the 1980s," 16–17.

11. McKnight, "Do No Harm," 7.

12. McKnight, "Regenerating Community," 48.

13. Susskind, "Resolving Environmental Disputes Through Ad Hocracy," 3.

14. Cousins, *Human Options*, 93.

15. Boyte, *Commonwealth*, 117.

16. Price and Flynn, "Alternative Democracy." See *Dayton Daily News*, February 2, 1992, 1A, February 3, 1992, 1A, 5A.

17. Graham, *Dynamic Managing*, 82–83.

18. Katz, "Neighborhood Politics," 49.

19. Ibid.

20. Boyte, "The Growth of Citizen Politics," 516.

21. Brecher and Costello, *Building Bridges*, 93.

22. Leo, "Community and Personal Duty."

23. Follett, *The New State*, 105.

24. Ibid., 40; emphasis in the original.

25. Hallett, "Communities Can Plan Future on Their Own Terms," 9.

26. Boyte, *Commonwealth*, 145–47.

27. See Mathews and McAfee, *Community Politics*, 9–12.

28. From the agencies' perspectives, the two programs have different targets. Health and Human Services is concerned with young people who need job training within the context of social services; Labor is concerned with people who just need skill enhancement in order to get a job. Personal communication with Fred Faris, Department of Health and Human Services, March 1992.

29. Personal communication with Fred Smith, retired chair and CEO of the Huffy Corporation, November 1991.

30. Gardner, "Building Community," 81.

31. Chrislip and Williams, *A Sense of Community*, 4.

32. Program for Community Problem Solving, *Community Problem Solving Case Summaries*, 5.

33. Weil, *Oppression and Liberty*, 86.

34. Hallett, "Communities Can Plan Future on Their Own Terms," 8.

35. See Yankelovich, *Coming to Public Judgment*. Yankelovich describes the evolution from public opinion to public judgment in three stages: consciousness raising, working through, and resolution.

36. For elaboration on the nature of choice work, see Mathews, McAfee, and McKenzie, *Hard Choices*, a handbook for people moderating NIF-type deliberations. It is available in Spanish and Russian, as well as in English.

37. Citizen juries are a special form of public deliberation designed by Ned Crosby's Jefferson Center in Minneapolis. See Raspberry, "Citizens' Juries."

38. National Association of Community Leadership Organizations, *Exploring Leadership*, 7–8.

39. Heifetz and Sinder, "Political Leadership," 179–202.

9

Marching to a Different Drummer: The Organization of Citizen Politics

Formal politics is highly organized. Organizations sit on top of organizations in ever-ascending hierarchical pyramids. Each one is filled with clerks, inspectors, executive directors, and just plain directors. Every agency comes complete with its own mandates, sets of regulations, and procedures. They respond to a welter of councils, legislative committees, and executive departments. The politics that people don't call politics—citizen politics—seems unorganized by comparison, but it isn't. It is just organized in different ways. The structures are different and what holds them together is different. They respond to different principles of management. Just as there is much to learn from the new thinking in citizen politics, there is also much to learn from the way citizen politics is organized.[1]

A great deal is being written these days about new ways of managing the country's business and industry so that we can compete more effectively in a world economy. Many of these principles for improving cooperation and productivity on the factory floor are identical to the new principles used in citizens' organizations. New thinking about public politics is like new thinking in management. Economic productivity begins, if it is to begin at all, on the shop floor. Political effectiveness begins, if it is to begin, on Main Street. The similarity of the concepts is not accidental. The early champions of citizens' organizations, like Mary Parker Follett, were also among the parents of the new business management theories. Both have deep roots in the American experience.

Public Space

Citizens' organizations create a special kind of political environment or "space" in a community. These organizations hold meetings where people can step back from their private and official roles and be public citizens. "Public spaces" are places in a community where people of diverse interests can come together to redefine their problems so they can come to a common understanding of the issues and determine an effective public response to them. Public space is space where everyone can feel he or she belongs. It is not anyone's territory.[2] The Wilowe Institute in Arkansas is an example of a citizens' organization that creates this type of space through public forums.

Dorothy Stuck, who had operated three weekly newspapers for twenty years in Arkansas, took a new look at the needs of her state when she returned from several years of service in the federal government. She was concerned about rapid changes that had moved Arkansas from its agrarian base to a service economy without much of an industrial period in-between. The state's communities and institutions did not appear to be responding well to change: education did not seem to be keeping pace; old racial divisions were still strong and destructive; communication channels were weak; cities and towns thrived or declined in isolation; and leadership was divided. In response, Dorothy Stuck joined with six other friends in 1982 to form a citizens' alliance that they named after a tree in her backyard—the Wilowe Institute. The institute's principal function is to convene citizens to deliberate on major policy issues facing the state as a whole.

Stuck and her colleagues believed the state needed the widest possible array of citizens to respond to its problems. Young people, those with little power or status, leaders of industry, state and local officials—everyone—needed to think together about their common future. As an expert on governmental organization, Stuck did not disdain government, but she knew there had to be more. Long-range planning and legislative study commissions, although useful, were not going to be enough. What was needed was an organization that could comprehend the relation among many issues and bridge the geographic, economic, and social barriers that divided the people of Arkansas.

One of the first brochures for the Wilowe Institute announced: "Many of us sense that vital social, economic, and political changes are beginning to affect our lives and the structures of our communities and state. Even so, few of us have found a means for sharing our reactions, our concerns, and especially our dreams for making those changes a positive force."[3] The institute was designed to offer an opportunity for such an exchange—to give citizens a forum for their voices and a place to develop their ideas. The institute's forums continue to attract a wide array of citizens to deliberate on the state's future. Their proudest claim is a list of new organizations and actions that have come out of their forums. Yet their greatest contribution may be the amount of public space they have created in Arkansas.

Associations

Chapter 7 reported on Americans' penchant for forming associations in order to work on common problems that affect their daily lives. The Wilowe Institute is such an association. Other associations manage the Naugatuck Valley project and the collaboration in Newark; associations are the principal organizational structure of citizen politics. These alliances of citizens are often ad hoc, temporary, and far less structured than the Associations that begin with a capital *A*, as in the "National Association for . . ." Citizens' associations range from committees to improve the schools, to alliances that promote neighborhood watches, to organizations that sponsor public forums.

Modern associations rest on a long tradition of civic associations in this country. In the United States we aren't collectivists; neither are we lone individualists, as we are sometimes portrayed. We are associationists; that is, we have a ready disposition to associate.[4] We are forever forming and joining associations with others who share our pastimes and interests. These informal organizations are the mediating institutions that serve as buffers between us and the mega-structures of government.[5] Early in our history, such visitors as Alexis de Tocqueville described this unique role of associations in American life:

> Americans of all ages, all stations in life, and all types of dispo-
> sition are forever forming associations. There are not only
> commercial and industrial associations in which all take part,
> but others of a thousand different types—religious, moral, se-
> rious, futile, very general and very limited, immensely large
> and very minute. Americans combine to give fêtes, found sem-
> inaries, build churches, distribute books, and send missionar-
> ies to the antipodes. . . . Finally, if they want to proclaim a
> truth or propagate some feeling by the encouragement of a
> great example, they form an association.[6]

Tocqueville was surprised to hear that a hundred thousand people in America had made a public promise not to drink alcoholic
beverages. Concerned about the effects of widespread drinking in
their communities, these citizens wanted others to associate with
them in this cause rather than each just privately "drinking water by
their own firesides." Tocqueville observed that, in France, the hundred thousand would have sent petitions asking the government to
regulate taverns.[7]

More than 150 years after Tocqueville made his observation, political analysts are still writing about associations, which now number in the thousands. Michael Novak, in his work on associations,
calls the people who form associations "communitarian individuals"
in order to make the point that they are connected to communities
as individuals but that the connection is through their many associations: "The spectrum of reality in America is broad, but a great
many Americans live quite rich communal, associative lives, both in
their families and at work, among friends they choose and among
others with whom fate has conjoined them."[8]

Of course, Americans are individualists in the sense that we see
the human being and not the collective whole at the center of our
democracy. We believe in the protection of human rights, the op-

portunity for each person to reach his or her full potential. Still, we have always been aware that individualism can become extreme and be at odds with the well-being of a community of individuals. So, as Novak notes, we have overcome extreme individualism by "the building up of many diverse associations and communities."[9]

The Community-Association Connection

American communities reflect a history of forming associations to solve political problems. Our communities were formed out of associations, and they survive through associations. Communities don't preexist people; people have to create them. Just because a community has been in a given location—Detroit or New York or Denver—doesn't mean that a community will always be there. It is only there if people continue to create associated life. It should not be surprising that the people in the Harwood discussions talked of their "community" as a set of associations. Associated life is the defining characteristic, or condition, of community life. Furthermore, community action through associations is the nonutopian way that Americans have always understood what democracy is all about.

The politics of problem solving is, as it always has been, associational politics. In associations, Americans come to understand—in practical, unabstract terms—what it means to be part of a public rather than just a mass of unassociated people.[10]

New Types of Associations

Throughout this country and all across the world, new forms of associations emerged during the last two decades of the century. Civic Forum, New Forum, and similar citizens' groups led the overthrow of communism in Eastern Europe. In Chile, Participa worked through a plebiscite to move the country toward a democratic regime. (Their slogan was "Democracy is everyone's responsibility.") Poder Ciudadano and Conciencia have begun to build a new civil society in Argentina. The Wilowe Institute and similar organizations have been created in the United States. These organizations are about problem solving and more; they are dedicated to changing the way politics operates, to changing the character of politics. Their creed is reflected in Vaclav Havel's words: "It is not that we should simply seek new and better ways of managing society, the economy and the world. The point is that we should fundamentally change how we behave."[11]

Of course, not all citizens' organizations have such long-term, fundamental objectives. More traditional ones have more circumscribed purposes. Advisory committees are useful in bringing public involvement to the work of formal institutions (parents' groups, for example, often advise schools). Advocacy groups have been effective in generating public support, as well as in bringing press attention to bear on agencies. Blue-ribbon committees of leading citizens have served to raise issues above partisan bickering. Partnership associations have brought organizations together for essential community work. They all make contributions.

In fact, these traditional forms of civic organization so dominate our experiences that we are sometimes unable to imagine other kinds of associations that are emerging—organizations open to all citizens and with a broad focus on the well-being of the community as a whole. These communitywide associations are a distinctive form of citizen organization.

The central idea of the communitywide organization is that the focus should be on the community in all its interrelations and connections, rather than on one specific issue. What sets this type of association apart from others is the notion that politics has more to do with the connections among a variety of problems than with certain particular problems. Associations of this kind have a broad, comprehensive outlook; they see their work as continuing over the long term. For example, when issues are being named and framed, communitywide associations come into being with the specific responsibility of seeing that essential connections are not lost.

Educational issues, for instance, are especially prone to be treated in isolation from other relevant community issues; they can be focused narrowly on the schools and on technical or professional considerations. When a community debates tax policy, it usually talks about taxes. But a debate over a school issue (such as the content of the curriculum or the state of discipline) can be badly misdirected. The question of the curriculum may be a surrogate for questions about economic strategies; the question of discipline in the schools may only be part of a larger question about how to maintain social order in the community. Issues that are so misframed can seldom be resolved, in part because the real parties to the debate often don't come to the table. For a community to address educational issues, those issues have to be put back into the context of community issues. That is the work of a citizens' organization like Wilowe.

Rather than advocating one set of interests or one particular solution, communitywide associations try to turn politics into an exercise in discovery. They look for the sources of community concern and the foundations of community strength. For them, politics is a search both for comprehensive definitions of their community's problems and for the capacity to solve them. This concept of their role keeps these associations from being overcome by the idea that their function is to press for specific outcomes to problems that are tightly defined. They see their mission as building community capability rather than just fixing specific problems.

Communitywide organizations are further distinguished by their concept of legitimacy, which is one of inclusiveness, not representativeness. People in these groups tend to participate as individual citizens, not as representatives of parties or organizations. The legitimacy of these associations depends on the breadth of their membership, their diversity. They are not necessarily large, but they are open. Their sense of politics also leads them to create alliances comprised of all those interested in contributing to the well-being of the community. They often refer to themselves as "boundary spanners" because of the importance they place on getting all of the stakeholders to the table.

Communitywide associations think of involvement as personal; people usually get a chance to do politics in a hands-on fashion. Staffs are small or nonexistent; much of the project work is done by the direct involvement of participants. One of their purposes is to combat the powerlessness of isolated individuals by building bonds among people. People's good intent, their impulse to tackle a problem, is easily lost, most often because people don't know that others share their concerns. Community associations are places where people can find one another; they are reservoirs for collecting political will.

These associations transform collective concerns into civic energy by encouraging people to join forces. By creating networks and partnerships, they build a set of relationships among civic organizations, a civic infrastructure that strengthens the political fabric of a community. They create channels for moving civic energy from one issue to another and from one group to another. And, by having members from many different organizations, they can stimulate collaborative, mutually reinforcing projects.

Different initiatives can be mutually reinforcing or complementary when they spring from a common set of purposes and are internally consistent. Communitywide associations, because of the way they are structured, have a chance to identify and create the commonness of purpose that is the basis for complementary action. This kind of action is the most effective action because the whole of the efforts is greater than the sum of the parts. Every initiative is magnified or amplified by the other initiatives that point in the same direction. We see complementary action when people who have worked together for a long time reinforce one another without direct supervision. An experienced surgical group, a seasoned football team, a skilled quartet of jazz musicians all work in a complementary way.

The structure and continuity provided by association can maintain the political momentum necessary for a community to stay with a problem long enough to treat its causes—not just its symptoms. A community association's job is to marshal ongoing support for those tasks that require patience and sacrifice. Crises quickly evoke popular support; support quickly dissipates once the crises are over. For fundamental, long-term problems, continuity is everything. Citizens' associations provide a measure of continuity simply by being around year after year.

In their relation to institutions and governments, community-wide associations see themselves as auxiliary, operating on a different but parallel plane of politics. They do not attempt to do the work of formal institutions. They do public work. Although their ties to institutions and governments can be close, they remain unofficial and informal. These organizations provide bridges between the public realm and the worlds of governments and institutions. They create laboratories where groups of people and groups of institutions can explore options outside the constraints of officialdom. They literally create circles (the typical seating arrangement in meetings) where people who work in the square boxes of hierarchical order can sit *around* one another and talk. This sort of rearrangement models new ways of relating politically; that is, the ways people learn to relate to one another and to common problems inside a citizens' association can become examples for trying new ways of relating outside these citizens' groups.

The Precepts of Associational Politics

Few have spelled out the ideas behind the politics of communitywide groups as well as Mary Parker Follett. Just after World War I, Follett sensed that newly organized interest groups could splinter government and turn politics into "war-like" contests. Although Americans had long lived by associations, by working together as neighbors and communities, that tradition was being tested by a diversity of new ideas and new people. Believing it essential for the tradition of community and associations to prevail, Follett argued that this new diversity should neither be celebrated nor avoided. It had to be used. And she thought that America's communities had a tradition of using diversity creatively. Communities seemed to her places where different people and groups came together to form a new whole. Not wanting differences to be eliminated by one group absorbing another, she put a premium on synthesizing diversity, which would lead to new and stronger forms of cooperation. She saw an ongoing process in which different elements of communities were constantly forming and then reforming themselves in new associations. Community politics, she believed, had to keep up this dynamic process of synthesis.

From Follett's perspective, community required creation, and that creation came through citizens interacting in associations with one another.[12] Merely consenting to be governed was not creative, nor would it produce a dynamic community. Follett thought that the new interest groups should learn to interact with other groups and not isolate themselves in their unique identity. The political chemistry of a community should not turn groups inward to protect their own interests but rather prepare them to turn outward, to form even more extensive associations. Consequently, communities had to remain places where people could learn how to associate.[13]

Covenants: The Force That Binds

Why do associations stick together when the problems they try to address are so frustrating? Battling street crime is not just time consuming; it is dangerous. Why does a whole neighborhood turn on its lights to defy drug dealers? Why do people show up to patrol crime-ridden streets? There is no financial or legal obligation requiring them to do what they do. People are not coerced into cooperating.

Associations are held together by a force that governments and institutions often find in short supply—the simple but powerful force of the promises people make to one another, their covenants. Covenants are the basis for community associations; they are the glue that holds them together and makes them work. In John McKnight's words, "The structure of institutions is a design established to create control of people. *The structure of associations is the result of people acting through consent.*"[14] We would be ill advised to forget about legal contracts, rules, regulations, and laws. Society can't rely totally on voluntary consent, but neither can it dismiss this time-honored way of banding together.

When citizens work in association with others, they do what is necessary: show up for a meeting, or canvass the neighborhood, or volunteer their time to coach Little League because they said they would and because others expect them to do what they say. These very informal agreements constitute voluntary covenants in which one party says to another, "We will do thus and so, if you will do thus and so." Although covenants may sound medieval or romantic, they work. They are not without their own kind of leverage. As one community leader said about his association's meetings, "If you don't show up, somebody will say something to you about it." The implicit promises people make to one another when they join in a common effort are usually honored because they are made in public before relative strangers, not forgiving family.

The first associations grew out of a need to increase cooperation among people. That is exactly why citizens turn to community associations these days—to do those things that no one can do alone. We don't use the word *covenant* much anymore, but we do use its Latin-derived equivalent, *federal*. We are still tied to the powerful tradition of covenants when we say that we have a federal government or when, in everyday speech, we call one another "pardner."[15] The parties to a covenant are partners.

Partnerships based on covenants are illustrated in associations like one in Dayton, Ohio, that brings predominantly black churches together with predominately white ones to work on such issues of common concern as adequate day care and the AIDS crisis. This joint venture is called the Vineyard project. The report of the initial meeting reads, "All present signed a covenant that affirmed their commitment" to one another and to the work they set out to do as partners.[16]

A covenant contains certain principles for structuring the way people work together. In covenants, the partnerships are voluntary; no one can be forced. Each party remains independent; no one is asked to merge his or her identity into some collective melting pot. People are not asked to bond with one another, or even to like one another. They just have to be willing to work together. The purpose or ends of the association have to be agreed upon mutually, so everyone has to have a say in what they are. The partners "own" the association; they are not employees or clients. Partners need not have equal resources. (After all, the first covenants were between God and humanity.) Yet, in civic partnerships everyone has to treat everyone else in the relationship as an equal. Why? Because everyone is dependent on the agreement of others, and everyone has a say in what the associations' purposes are.[17]

When Americans rely on covenants to create associations, they are following a well-established political practice. The first American covenant created the early New England community. It was made while people were still at sea aboard the *Mayflower*. Their mutual promises are clear in the language of the Mayflower Compact, which reminds us that communities are essentially "civic bodies politic": "In the name of God, Amen. We whose names are under written . . . Having undertaken for the Glory of God, and Advancement of the Christian Faith, and the Honour of our King and Country, a Voyage to plant the first colony in the northern Parts of Virginia; Do by these Presents, solemnly and mutually in the Presence of God and one another, covenant and combine ourselves together into a civil Body Politik,—for our better Ordering and Preservation, and Furtherance of the Ends aforesaid."[18]

Daniel Elazar, who has written a history of covenants, found that the process of creating community by covenants continued throughout the settlement of the country. Covenants also affected American politics in other ways. Elazar notes that covenantal principles were "extended into most areas of human relationship, shaping American notions of individualism, human rights and obligations, social expectations, business organization, civic association, and church structure."[19]

Covenantal principles, which were at the heart of our self-governing associations, eventually worked their way into our state and national constitutions. John Adams used the concepts of the Mayflower Compact of 1620 when he wrote a preamble to the Massachusetts Constitution in 1779:

The body politic is formed by a voluntary association of individuals. It is a social compact by which the whole people covenants with each citizen and each citizen with the whole people, that all shall be governed by certain laws of the common good. It is the duty of the people, therefore, in framing a Constitution of Government, to provide for an equitable mode of making laws, as well as for an impartial interpretation and a faithful execution of them, that every man may, at all times, find his security in them.[20]

When Covenants Are Broken

Covenantal principles still are central to all of American politics. Citizens not only make covenants to form associations, but
their relation to governments is also based on covenantal principles.
We, the people, agree to do certain things if they, the government,
will do certain things. Actually, in the United States, the implicit
covenant between the people and the government has two parts.
The first part says that the people will do their duty (such as vote or
pay taxes) if the government provides services. Essentially the same
understanding exists in most countries. Ours, however, is a democratic country, so the second and most important part of our covenant is that the people will do their duty if the government is also
responsive to public direction. Americans are angry at the political
system now because they believe the most essential part of their
covenant with government has been broken. Breaking a covenant is
more than a passing political dyspepsia. A broken covenant threat-
ens the foundations of a political order.

In 1978, long before the Main Street study was done, Elazar pre-
dicted the present public hostility because he saw that the covenant
was in jeopardy. Perceptively, he wrote, "Today Americans are confronted with the obvious failure of hierarchial structures which are
not only unable to 'deliver the goods,' but which have even come to
distort delivery systems" to meet their own ends.[21] At the same
time, the role of citizen degenerated from that of a participator who
has definite responsibilities to other citizens and his or her polity to
that of a consumer in a marketplace of service delivery systems.

Notes

1. A description of citizen-based politics can be found in Mathews and
McAfee, *Community Politics.*
2. See Evans and Boyte, *Free Spaces.*
3. Stuck, "The Wilowe Institute," 1.
4. Novak, "Mediating Institutions," 4–9.
5. Ibid.
6. Tocqueville, *Democracy in America,* 513.

7. Ibid., 516.
8. Novak, "Mediating Institutions," 8.
9. Ibid.
10. Dewey, *The Public and Its Problems*, 185.
11. Havel, "The End of the Modern Era."
12. Follett, *The New State*, 7.
13. Ibid., 147.
14. McKnight, "Regenerating Community," 48, emphasis added.
15. Elazar and Kincaid, "Covenant and Polity," 6.
16. Vineyard Project, *The Vineyard* [newsletter], 3.
17. Elazar and Kincaid, "Covenant and Polity," 4–8.
18. Elazar, "America and the Federalist Revolution," 67.
19. Ibid.
20. Ibid.
21. Elazar, "Harmonizing Government Organization," 56.

Part 5

What Is Politics and Who Owns It?

Our constitution . . . favors the many instead of the few; this is why it is called a democracy. . . . Our public men have, besides politics, their private affairs to attend to, and our ordinary citizens, though occupied with the pursuits of industry, are still fair judges of public matters; for, unlike any other nation, [we regard] him who takes no part in these duties not as unambitious but as useless, . . . and instead of evoking discussion as a stumbling block in the way of action, we think it an indispensable preliminary to any action at all.

—Pericles

10

Responding to the Critics

After reading the accounts of what citizens are doing in the Wilowe Institute and the National Issues Forums and the Lake Union project—and in all of the other places where people are practicing citizen politics—it is time to return to the question posed in the Introduction: Is optimism about ordinary people's ability to decide on their common future justified? Are people up to the intellectual and moral demands of democratic citizenship, or are they too uninformed or too selfish to pursue anything other than their parochial interests? Is citizen politics, at its best, essentially defensive, most likely used to keep drug treatment centers out of a neighborhood or block the location of a garbage incinerator? Are the conditions of modern life so complex and overwhelming that mere citizens are no match for the centralized forces said to control their lives?

Many Americans, even some who have doubts about the public, would like evidence that these charges against the citizenry can be refuted. They would like to believe that a vital community spirit is alive in the country, that citizens are smarter than they are given credit for being, and that people's self-interests incorporate their social interests. They would like to believe that citizens are willing to devote time to serious deliberation on the issues and that public deliberation can influence what politicians and governments do. They would like to be hopeful, and they want something concrete to sustain their hope. So they ask, "Are the people quoted in this book real; are the projects that were described representative? Tell us more. Help us convince those who seem unaware of what citizens can do—and actually do—on their own behalf."

It is tempting to try to answer these questions on their own terms, to add more examples and case studies. Unfortunately, the evidence is always contradictory. For every positive example there is a counterexample. The fact of the matter is that facts alone will not make the case for citizen politics. But there are reasonable responses to the questions that citizen politics raises.

Can People Measure Up to the Demands of Democratic Citizenship?

Stories about people who don't do their civic duty are easy to find. In the same year that saw record turnouts for national elections, only four out of every hundred eligible voters in Jefferson Township, Ohio, made the decision that the police and fire departments would have to do without additional funds.[1] In Dutton, Alabama, at about the same time, the governor had to appoint a town council because no one ran for any of the five seats.[2]

Those who defend democracy have to face up to unpleasant realities, to the forces that lead people away from active and responsible citizenship. No one can say for sure how many Americans will take time for highly organized civic activities. Neither do we know how much people express their citizenship in everyday activities rather than in formal programs. Still, the public's response to public forums, study circles, and citizen juries suggests that conventional wisdom badly underestimates the number of people who will act, in some way, on their citizenship. And we can be reasonably certain that the participation of some prompts the participation of more.

Americans are subject to conflicting influences that can immobilize even those who genuinely want to participate in constructive change. People want change in the economy, in the health-care system, in the educational system, and in the political system. Change was so much in the air just before the 1992 elections that all candidates embraced it—even the incumbents. Speaking for many others, a citizen in California said, "I hope we're going to get a change. . . . I don't care who gets in there. I just hope we do some changing around in this country because it can't go on like it is right now."[3] Yet these very people who want change so badly can be a major obstacle to reform.

Some are afraid to take the initiative and make the sacrifices that change requires, even though the risks are relatively low in this country compared to the risks that, for example, reformers in Eastern Europe have taken. At times, Americans are afraid of other Americans; they are afraid of being ripped off by the greedy and self-serving. While change requires risk taking, this fear promotes just the opposite—defensiveness. Some wait for permission to work for change, although change requires claiming responsibility and not waiting for permission. Some want change but also want to feel secure and to be cared for. Change, however, means living with feelings of uncertainty and insecurity. Some impose conditions on their becoming politically engaged and working for change. They say that they are waiting for trust and fairness to be established before they do anything political, not recognizing that politics is about establishing fairness and that it takes involvement to build confidence among people. Some know they have to deal with the substantive issues that change entails, yet they are easily distracted from the difficult choices by tales of waste, fraud, and abuse. Although there is real waste, fraud, and abuse, it is not the primary problem in many issues. The rising cost of health care, for example, is not primarily due to waste, fraud, and abuse.[4] Blaming others can be an excuse for inaction.

In the face of such resistance, how do we ever manage to change? Is it only those who don't have such fears and hesitations that make the changes? No. The people who changed the living conditions in Cochran Gardens and rebuilt the economy of the Naugatuck Valley and arrested the decline of Newark had these same reservations. They were uncertain and apprehensive. They didn't cease to be afraid; they just added something else to the equation—a sense of possibility, a belief that if they acted, they might make a difference.

Can Citizens Transcend Their Self-Interests? Do They Need To?

Beyond the question of whether people are inclined to take part in politics, there is the question of whether people are suited for politics—whether their interest in the larger good is just a superficial gloss over deeper parochial motivations. As noted in chapter 3, there are those who try to work for the common good, whether out of selflessness or out of an understanding that their own interests will suffer if the commonweal is ignored. But what about all those other instances, some ask, when people only take part in politics to protect their own narrow interests—regardless of the toll on others? Sometimes it seems that people are roused out of their private lives and into the public arena only to protect themselves.

This phenomenon is so common it even has an acronym: NIMBY, for "not in my backyard." The term *NIMBY* describes those instances when people who may have never taken part in politics suddenly become politically animated because of a perceived threat: "We don't care where you put the garbage incinerator as long as you don't put it in *our* neighborhood." Despite the simple acronym, the NIMBY phenomenon is very complicated. To be sure, some people start out in politics because of a threat to their own backyard and continue in politics to help others in similar situations. A NIMBY reaction may also be due to some people's genuine displeasure at bearing a disproportionate amount of risk without adequate safeguards or compensation. Nevertheless, many onlookers say that NIMBY is a perfect illustration of people's inherent selfishness.

The NIMBY phenomenon raises the question of whether citizens, under pressure, are bound to understand their self-interest narrowly. To begin with, the unstated assumption that these self-interests have to be "transcended" is open to question. Chapter 8 was full of stories about people who used self-interests to realize a common good. The Newark Collaboration is a case in point. The Lake Union project presents even more interesting evidence that self-interests can be the building blocks of a comprehensive strategy for problem solving. You will recall that the coalition to preserve the lake was based on connecting the self-interests of the people who lived along the shoreline: houseboat owners, the owners of small businesses, and environmentalists. Like James Madison, the people of Lake Union appreciated the reality of self-interests, yet they also went beyond Madison. He only thought of using one interest to block another; they thought of joining interests.

The NIMBY phenomenon is actually evidence of what happens when there is too little rather than too much citizen politics. Some policy decisions will inevitably make for inequitable distributions of burdens and gains. People near a hazardous materials dump will necessarily bear more risk than their neighbors in the next county. Still, all of their self-interests do not have to be sacrificed. And the same people must not always bear the greatest burden in every decision. It is imperative to see all of the self-interests in a community and to both connect and balance them. Citizen politics, which is an inclusive politics for making connections with others, is an antidote to narrow parochialism.

While some citizens come to act in the public interest because they believe it to be in their self-interest, others come at the matter from just the opposite direction. They believe the community's interests are the sum of its citizens' self-interests. To them, self-interests are good, and the more they are articulated, the better the community's solutions will be. They argue that "self-interest, expressed through participation, is the basis for identifying and meeting community interests."[5] Problem solving is, by these lights, finding the connections, the common threads, the overlapping concerns, the trade-offs among diverse self-interests.

People who become involved in community projects nearly always say that they began with issues that affected their self-interests. A woman from Little Rock explained her support of an anti-crime program: "I literally found syringe needles and stuff lying [by] the side of my house," she reported. "I said, my God, I've got to do something; I can't go to bed here at night knowing that this is going on in my driveway."[6]

This comment is particularly telling because it not only shows that people have to have a personal stake in an issue before they will become politically active, but it also shows that self-interests are constantly evolving. As our sense of self changes with experience, so does our self-interest. Participation prompts this change. As Yvonne Sims says of a decade of involvement in the National Issues Forums in Grand Rapids, Michigan, "The experience has changed me." And, as she changed, so did her self-interests.[7]

Self-interests are "constructs"; people decide (construe) either wisely or unwisely that something is in their self-interest. People can always change these conclusions. What is constructed can be reconstructed.

Civic participation—what we do as citizens—prompts us to reconsider our self-interests, often to broaden our definition of those self-interests. Why? The generic question we always confront as citizens is, in one form or another, What should we do as a community? To answer that question we look at all of our interests, all of our concerns and convictions, and all of our experiences. We don't want to miss anything.

When we ask how any proposal or policy will affect me, we mean, How will this affect all that I care about? Our focus is broad rather than narrow. Broadening our definition of self-interest seems to begin with a conversation or a telling experience.

A woman said that her interest in the health problems of the homeless began with emotional problems her son was having. Another became involved in the literacy movement because of the troubling experience of graduating from high school with peers who could not read. In all of these situations there were catalysts that stimulated making connections—a neighbor who shared his concerns about water rights, a young person who asked about the environment, a relative stranger in a public forum who added a different perspective on what had seemed a nonissue.[8] As Ernesto Cortes has said of his career in community work, "You begin to see your interests as broadening in relationships with other people, particularly as you begin to have serious conversations and you begin to identify with other people's experiences."[9]

The point is that when we respond to questions about self-interest, we often think of them as static and forget about this capacity for civic learning and redefining our interests. People are capable of more than the simple deduction that their immediate and present interests are affected by what happens to a common good. We can learn and mature politically just as we can mature intellectually and socially. Our sense of what is in our present interest changes along the way. For example, Joan Martin-Brown, associate regional director for North America of the United Nations Environment Program, explained her global interests as a natural evolution of her self-interests. Once limited to her hometown, her concern about the environment grew to include her state and country, and then came to encompass the environment of the planet.[10] Perhaps this evolution is driven by an expanding sense of what matters over time. Biologists explain this phenomenon as "long-term selfish interests."[11]

The problem comes when we stop looking over our backyard fences and close our eyes to all that is affecting us. Then we stop seeing connections. What makes citizen politics an effective counter to this problem is its ability to take people into one another's backyard. People who put up fences to define what is theirs can also pull them down when they see how much what they thought was theirs is affected by what lies outside their initial boundaries. Their backyards get larger. After an especially difficult forum on racial problems and affirmative action, one African-American participant spoke about what the issue might look like from a white person's "backyard": "I guess if I were a white man . . . and somebody came along and said that there are scarce resources and everybody won't be able to get the same if we give so-and-so the chance, I would think that I might be one of those people [who] might not get a chance."[12]

Do Citizens Have the Means to Be Effective?

Citizen politics relies heavily on deliberation to get people out of their own backyards—and beyond their parochial perspectives. One person's story connects with another person's experience. We take in the experience of the other and our world becomes larger.

Despite these strengths, however, all kinds of charges are leveled against public deliberation.[13] One major criticism is that citizens making deliberative choices can't guarantee that their decisions will be put into immediate action, so they have no real power.

Actually, the charge that deliberation cannot guarantee action is well founded. Deliberation was never thought to be all that was necessary for wise public action. As Pericles said almost 2,500 years ago, deliberation is only a preliminary form of action, a necessary but not sufficient condition for getting results. The function of public deliberation is to increase the chances that any action that follows will be sound; that is, that people will have thought out the consequences of their actions before they take them (as much as consequences can ever be anticipated before an action). Deliberation does not guarantee action; rather, it creates the possibility that an action will be taken mindful of the consequences. Deliberation helps us look before we leap.

Deliberation is also criticized when it is misunderstood. Two neighborhood activists wanted to use what they considered deliberation to secure local control of a nearby decommissioned military base. They took their request to city and federal officials and attempted to "deliberate" with them. When they weren't successful, they reasoned that deliberation was just talk and politically ineffective. Obviously, what happened is that the neighborhood leaders had begun with a solution, not an open issue with several alternatives for action. Deliberation is a way of making a decision; it is of no use when a decision has already been made.

What is more, the real issue in this case was never addressed. What the neighborhood really wanted was to revitalize its economy and improve living conditions. There were a number of ways to reach that objective. Getting control of the military base was only one—and one that was not without some negative consequences. Old bases are costly to remodel and costly to maintain.

The most essential part of deliberation is deciding on the nature of the issues and all of the possible alternatives for addressing them. Although deliberation ends in choice work—in struggling to find the most suitable options—it begins by framing issues for public examination. In a rush to solutions, it is easy to overlook the way an issue is framed. But the way a problem is framed almost predetermines the kind of solution we will find and whether there will be any shared sense of purpose. It also affects who will be drawn to solving the problem and the amount of public will that will be generated. Deliberation, despite the criticisms and misapplications, appeals to people because it opens up the framing of issues and because it builds common purpose and political will.

Americans worried that the country is adrift are particularly sensitive to the importance of shared purposes as a prerequisite for solutions. Solutions spring up out of the morning news like grass after a summer shower, but shared objectives are harder to come by. Public deliberation is valued because it allows people to articulate shared interests and purposes, which are the common ground needed for effective action. In communities where groups hold National Issues Forums, for example, their objective is to build this kind of common ground—especially on issues on which full agreement is impossible.

Take the problems that put young people at risk in America— and the fragmentation of political effort described in chapter 8. Communities like Sumter, South Carolina, and Englewood, New Jersey, have used deliberative forums to arrive at common purposes that, in turn, have sparked complementary action throughout the communities. After forums on the issue of growing up at risk, citizens used action workbooks to see whether they had a shared sense of the problems and to come up with a statement of purpose that most everyone could live with. Reaching a shared sense of the problems implies—but only implies—a common set of purposes. Actually describing those purposes was quite a struggle. As one participant said, "It took four or five tries for people to come up with a statement of purpose that they could agree on."[14] Reaching some accord by hammering out a statement seemed to prompt a commitment to act together. With common goals, people were able to do more than act unilaterally. What one group did was reinforced by what another did.

But do the choices citizens make in public forums influence more than other citizens? Do they influence the positions that politicians and governments take on issues? Usually, people asking these questions want an unqualified yes or no answer. The reality is that although public choices can affect policy-making, they rarely do so overnight—and for good reason. Most political issues, even the economic situation of one small community, take time to understand, plan for, and act on. That is why the most successful democratic action is deliberative. On major national issues, it can take a decade or more to change politics. The role of deliberation is to keep that long journey on track and out of unproductive complaining and blaming. Deliberation is not good at quick fixes; it is more likely to be used to recover from them.

The price deliberation pays for doing its job is high; people doubt its ability to affect policy because they are looking for immediate responses in what is necessarily a slow process. Does public deliberation eventually affect official policy-making? There is evidence that it does. Fortunately, we have Page and Shapiro's longitudinal study of fifty years of public opinion—opinion they found to be shaped by deliberation.[15] They cited issues around which public opinion developed independently from government policy and paved the way for a change in that policy. For instance, the gradual change toward favoring more pragmatic relations with what was once called Red China shows how public opinion anticipated what Presidents Nixon and Carter would do two decades later.

Officials, like former Secretary of State Dean Rusk, have no difficulty believing in the cumulative power of public opinion and the inability of the government to sustain long-term policy without public support. In Rusk's words, "At the end of the day, the American people are going to have to decide. No president can pursue a policy for very long without the support and the understanding of the Congress and the American people. That's been demonstrated over and over again."[16] On issues that citizens care about deeply, there is usually a "rather high congruence" between official positions and the views of the public.[17]

How Much Can We Rely on the Public's Opinions?

Any evidence that public opinion does affect policy-making leads to another worry: Is it really good for policy to be swayed by popular reactions? Can we be confident that people will actually deliberate enough to know what they are talking about or be realistic in their expectations? Consider the issue of health care, where people want more coverage but don't expect to pay more for it. In 1992, although acutely conscious of their out-of-pocket costs, most Americans were unaware of the factors that drove those costs (like advanced medical technology) and who paid for them. Citizens believed that they paid for more than 70 percent of the costs directly through their insurance, whereas, in fact, they paid for less than 30 percent.[18] Obviously, we should not depend on opinion that is so ill informed. Yet, neither should we make too much of this case. In 1992, the country was just beginning an intensive debate on health-care costs, and people were in the early stages of dealing with the consequences of expanding coverage.

Early on in the life of a policy debate, opinions are likely to be ill formed and unstable. As people first become aware of an issue, reactions tend to be based on initial impressions and poor information. Opinions fluctuate almost from day to day. Becoming aware of an issue, as Daniel Yankelovich points out, is a long way from the point where public judgment is stable, coherent, and forceful. There are many obstacles along the way—such as blaming others and engaging in wishful thinking to avoid the hard decisions. To develop mature public judgment, Yankelovich says, people have to explore a variety of choices; they have to overcome a natural resistance to facing costly trade-offs; they have to look honestly at all the pros and cons; and, finally, they have to take a stand, both intellectually and emotionally.[19] It is a long journey.

In the aggregate and over time, when popular opinion becomes more reflective and shared, the public does seem to know what it is talking about. Page and Shapiro, you will recall, found that collective judgment is "rational" and "reflects a considerably higher level of information and sophistication than is apparent at the individual level."[20] What makes this difference between popular opinion and public judgment? Deliberation, the same thing it takes to make a population a public.

Outcomes of National Issues Forums around the country have shown that deliberation can blend individual voices into more inclusive and reasoned "public voices."[21] Deliberation prompts people to look at the costs of what may, at first, seem exactly the right course of action. In 1991 in forums on freedom of expression, people reacted strongly against what they saw as an invasion of pornography. Yet as they weighed the consequences of restricting expression, especially when they considered the prospects of government controls, they moved from their initial outrage to a more balanced response. They became increasingly reluctant to have the government interfere, although they remained troubled that unwelcomed expression (pornography) could invade their lives without their having a chance to turn it off.[22]

In this and other instances, deliberation encourages us to consider all that is truly valuable. Our attitudes change when we see that every issue touches on more than one of our concerns. So we aren't disposed to give one value absolute priority over another; we are more likely to look for a course of action that respects several values. And we become much more aware of the importance of the circumstances or context that bears upon a decision. Rather than resolving the tension among values with one-size-fits-all decrees, we are more likely to respond case by case.

That happened in the forums on freedom of expression. This issue, like many others, is usually framed around just one value and presented as a contest between good and evil. Everything is depicted as black or white; there are no shades of gray. People in deliberations tend to reject that kind of framework as too simple. Deliberation brings back the complexity. Forum participants approached the issue as one in which several values were at stake—both the individual freedom to speak and the individual freedom to choose what one is exposed to. As they worked their way through the issue, they did not favor one value at the expense of the other; they respected the tension between them. So they did not favor a universal, national policy but rather local, case-by-case decisions about specific problems in specific circumstances.

Although reflective deliberation is usually thought of as the opposite of action, on certain issues forums seem to move people to act sooner and with more resolve than might otherwise be the case. The 1991 National Issues Forums also dealt with energy policy. In discussions on that issue, people shifted from thinking of finding long-term energy sources as a distant problem to seeing it as a critical issue. So they became much more inclined to support changes in policy and to consider changes in the way they used energy.

Deliberation on this issue was particularly interesting because the subject was full of scientific and technical considerations, which are supposed to overwhelm average citizens who have little scientific or technical expertise. However, on this and other issues of similar complexity, forum participants were not the least overwhelmed. Although complaining about the lack of information on some options and conflicting information on others, they had little difficulty in assessing the pros and cons of renewable sources of energy—including nuclear power.

Another quite different piece of evidence points to the same conclusion: Even on highly technical issues, deliberative public judgment is not inferior to the judgment of scientists. The public is far more capable of sound judgments on technical issues than it is given credit for. The evidence comes from a study done by the Public Agenda Foundation with Gerald Holton and Marcel LaFollette of Harvard University. Approximately seventy participants, statistically representative of the general public, were polled for their opinions on a number of research projects involving complex technical issues. Six groups of about a dozen participants each were then given information about the projects and took part in a deliberative discussion. When asked at the end of the meetings for their judgment on the projects, there were surprisingly few differences be-

tween the judgments of those who were knowledgeable about science and those who were not once they had all had a chance to reflect on and talk about all the options.[23]

Although there are, indeed, experts on questions of fact, there is
no such thing as experts on policy questions, which are really questions of "what should we do?" Experts are no more competent than
anyone else on "should" questions; their competence is on questions of how to do what we believe we should do.

On these complex scientific issues and on issues that have difficult trade-offs, such as affordable health care, it should not be surprising that the public needs time to work its way through tough
decisions. After all, we expect courts, legislatures, and executive
bodies to be deliberative. Why should we prescribe anything different for the public?

Does Citizen Politics Really Work?

In considering the question of whether people are really capable of self-government, here is the "evidence" so far: people can
overcome the barriers to active citizenship. Self-interests are not
necessarily impediments to advancing the common good. Many
citizens are willing to deliberate with their fellow citizens, and, if
that deliberation has proceeded long enough, people can really
know what they are talking about. Deliberation can give purpose
to citizen action and broad direction to government policy. The
unexplored question, however, is whether it always—or even usually—follows that deliberative politics carries the day. Does citizen politics really work?

It is undeniable, even when deliberation succeeds in defining a
shared interest and the public decides on a common direction for
action, that other political forces can overwhelm citizen politics.
Robin Lambert, who has spent a decade in small, rural communities in Alabama—working to help them keep their schools open and
their economies stable—knows all too well how citizens' best efforts can be defeated.[24] She recalls a school board that closed three
rural schools over citizens' protests because the county's largest in-

dustry wanted the buildings and believed consolidation made the county system more cost efficient. Neither the facts about the effectiveness of rural schools, the superior academic record of their graduates, nor the disadvantages of added transportation costs and crowding had any effect. The citizens trying to save their schools had a hard time just getting a conversation going. Those in authority only wanted to address the problems in their own terms. Although the citizens laid out their concerns and presuppositions, the officials were unwilling to do the same. So the citizens' efforts were stymied. People in other communities have similar stories to tell.

In these situations, people often feel overwhelmed by centralized powers that control decision making. These experiences give rise to the conclusion that citizens really aren't strong enough to control their own future, that citizen politics is relatively powerless.

Yet, even in situations where people appear helpless, there can be amazing stories of citizen power. For instance, the officials who rejected the proposal to give the military base to the neighborhood did not totally control the economic future of the neighborhood. As John McKnight has suggested, the most important economic resources in any situation are people's talents and their ability to work together toward common objectives.[25] Citizens are in control of those resources, which grow out of their own capacities. Politically, when citizens rename problems and frame issues in their own terms, they increase their power. And when they come up with options that go beyond the conventional ones, they are better able to counter the convergence of external forces that would otherwise drive policy decisions.

This type of citizen power and its effect can be seen in projects such as the one that helped citizens of Des Moines, Iowa, set health policy for their community. The problem there, as in many cities, was the rising cost of good care. Although Des Moines hasn't completely eliminated what is clearly a nationwide problem, the situation has improved as a result of the role the public played. Project leaders had the issue reframed to lay out all the options and explain what was at stake in terms of what people considered valuable. As more than two hundred public forums challenged the community to face up to the hard choices that had to be made, the media ran stories on the issue, reaching 76 percent of the residents. Nearly half of the area's adult population read the special supplement in the *Des Moines Register*, and more than thirty thousand responded to a special "ballot" on the choices.[26]

Throughout the campaign, public understanding of the issue grew. By the end of it, people knew they had to act. They did not decide on just one plan and one solution; there were many, and they complemented one another. The community's first health maintenance organization opened with greater participation than expected. Hospitals reduced their number of rooms and offered a variety of new outpatient services. The state legislature passed a bill to allow insurance coverage for these services. Due to these and other efforts, insurance rates in Iowa dropped by 5 percent.[27] Similar cases can be found throughout the country. Communities are trying "community-based" strategies for change or "community-based" solutions. They are getting results through people.[28]

Is the Public Really Necessary?

Des Moines seems a wonderful case of citizens in action, but how much does it prove? Does it prove that citizen politics is the only way to get a bill passed or change policy? Of course not. There are cases where cities have acted decisively on problems with little or no public involvement.

In the early 1980s, faced with the all-too-familiar "problem" of multiple local jurisdictions with conflicting goals, business leaders in Battle Creek, Michigan, tried to persuade the city and township governments to merge. Not surprisingly, township residents opposed the consolidation. Then a major business threatened to move its headquarters to a new area unless there was a merger. That "solved" the problem. Fearing a loss of seven hundred jobs, the township voted itself out of existence. The public participated but only to ratify the plan for consolidation laid down by the business interests. Despite charges of blackmail by some, the majority of city and township residents seemed pleased that a solution had been reached to a long-standing dispute.[29]

The contrast between these vignettes from Des Moines and Battle Creek doesn't justify overall conclusions about any differences there may be in the two cities. After all, only two events are at issue. Still, placing the situations side by side raises the question of whether the public—even if competent—is really necessary for political problem solving. Our original question of whether we are entitled to be optimistic about the public has become a larger and more complex question. With effective polling methods and sophisticated techniques for selling solutions to the public, why bother with the slow and messy business of public deliberation and involving citizens?

There are several ways of responding to this question. The first begins by looking at the type of problem being addressed. One noticeable difference between the Des Moines case and the situation in Battle Creek is that the issues were not the same. The issue in Battle Creek was how to organize government for greater efficiency. The issue in Des Moines was how to address a systemic problem—the rising cost of good health care. It may be that certain kinds of problems require more from the public than do others.

Ronald Heifetz, a physician now teaching government at Harvard University, knows from his background that there are significant differences in types of problems and that these differences require different remedies. Medical problems range from those that are routine and can be cured by a physician to more serious ones where the diagnosis is not clear-cut and there are no technical fixes. Think of the difference between a broken arm and diabetes; there is a technical remedy for the former but not the latter. For the most serious problems, the patient and physician have to combine forces. Similarly, our most serious political problems are those where the very definition of the problem is unclear and the nature of the treatment undefined. These are political problems that governments and their experts can't fix by themselves. Without a responsible public engaged, there is little hope of healing.[30] This principle of citizen politics was summed up well by the editor of the *Wichita Eagle*, Davis Merritt: "The only way . . . for the community to be a better place to live is for the people of the community to understand and accept their personal responsibility for what happens."[31]

This is not to say that the public and its deliberations are only appropriate for extremely complex issues. The public can be found at work on exceedingly ordinary problems, with benefits that go beyond an immediate solution.

In Oxford, Ohio, the Environmental Protection Agency closed the local landfill, which was filled to capacity. Initially, the local government contracted to have all the community's garbage collected and trucked out of town. Many people, however, were interested in solving the problem rather than just shipping it somewhere else, so citizens began to discuss the issue in public meetings. The community deliberated. The press ran stories. And the city council responded to the issue. Finally, a decision was reached that required both public and governmental action. Citizens had to sort their trash by pulling out the recyclable material, and the town council had to find a contractor who would pick up both types of garbage.[32] The town solved at least a part of the problem, and the citizens were very much a part of the solution.

While many communities have begun recycling programs without such public involvement, sorting the garbage wasn't all that happened in Oxford. People increased their skills in solving problems together, skills that might be useful for issues more complex than removing trash—issues where no town council could decree a solution, where no leading institution could prescribe the resolution, issues that would require the commitment of public will and even public sacrifice. Those working for cleaner water in the Tennessee River understood this capacity building when they said, in effect, "We have become the solution." No solution in politics is more than temporary; the real measure of a community is its ability to adapt constantly to new situations. That is why building civic capacity ("becoming the solution") is, in the long run, more important than finding today's solution.

Today's solution could well be tomorrow's problem. But who will be willing to say so? Today's solutions become institutionalized in bureaucracies, laws, and power structures. And even the most well-intentioned of the "powers that be" are often the least likely to recognize when change is necessary. The way Oxford went about solving its problems helped establish a practice that promotes self-correction. That is to say, a strong argument for a citizen's democracy is not that the people will always make the best decision about the future but that self-government is the most likely to be self-corrective.

When people accept "personal responsibility for what happens," it both creates the potential for self-corrective action and expands the range of what is possible in politics. Citizens would say that is what makes them really necessary.

Can We Count on a Civic Responsibility?

So people have to claim their responsibility. The real question continues to be, Will they? People will act responsibly when they see a possibility that they can get their hands on a problem and make a difference. But what happens when there is considerable doubt about whether anyone can make a difference?

Clearly, the conviction that people should be responsible does not lead to an equal certainty that citizens will be effective when they act on their responsibilities. The doubts never go away. Civic leaders who have succeeded in making a difference nearly always report that they had to face serious doubts about their effectiveness. Even their closest allies were skeptical at one time or another.[33] In part, the skepticism grows out of an inability to see immediate effects from efforts to make the structural changes for which many citizen initiatives aim. Although common sense tells us that solutions begin with citizens banding together, we are impatient for tangible results. What seems to prompt people to act as citizens in the face of skepticism and doubt is the fear that if people don't try, don't get involved, things will most surely get worse. This deep-seated conviction that the country will be far worse off if citizens don't try to make a difference is reflected in such comments as, "I'm an American citizen, so I'm part of the solution or I'm part of the problem. . . . You can't be in limbo."[34] In other words, if people don't try to make a difference, that itself becomes the overriding problem.

Another, more positive, motivation is that more than a few

Americans prefer to live the life of citizens. To be sure, some are happy to delegate to government agencies and major institutions as much of the task of managing their communities and the country as they can. Many others, however, want to live in communities, and a country, where citizens set the direction and do their fair share of the common work. They want the government to do its job, and yet they want to be more than clients and consumers. As the leader of the Naugatuck project said about the importance of citizens working together to solve common problems, if citizens are busy being citizens, then a city is by definition a better place to live.[35] Many of us like to live in communities of "people who get things done."[36]

The Claims of Citizen Politics

Having spoken to many of the particular questions about citizens and their capacities, what can now be said, overall, to the claims of those who believe that citizen politics is right, necessary, and possible? What are we being asked to believe?

Certainly we are not being asked to believe that the evidence compels us to be optimistic about democracy in the way that facts compel us to believe the earth is round, not flat. Yet, in the absence of conclusive evidence, is citizen politics based on no more than a belief; is it simply a matter of faith?

Not at all. We have a great deal of experience, historical and contemporary, to sustain at least a cautiously optimistic view of people's capacity for self-government. Democracy works in some places and in some situations today. In the past it worked in New England town meetings, Swiss cantons, and Greek city-states.[37]

That being said, democracy's claim is not based primarily on historical experience; it is based on the proposition that democracy is a "realizable ideal." At first that may appear to be contradictory, but only if we think ideals exclude reality and that reality excludes ideals. Here is what the claim means: A political ideal, by definition, always exceeds reality. It always leads us beyond where we are, paving the way to what might be. That is fine as long as the ideal doesn't mislead—doesn't point us to something that can never be. We have to be able to experience, at least in part, what the ideal tells us is possible.[38]

The people cited in this book have actually experienced a measure of the democratic ideal in practice. To be sure, those experiences were always bittersweet, always incomplete. People in National Issues Forums, for example, often say, "We really enjoy talking this way" (meaning deliberatively). Then they quickly add, "Why don't we do this more often?" Or they worry, "Will what we have said make any difference?" The experience of democracy is always partial—and necessarily so—because the democratic ideal is always challenging democratic practice.

What, then, are these citizens asking us to believe? Simply that what they have experienced can be experienced by others; that if deliberation can happen in one meeting, it can happen in others; that if citizens can claim responsibility and act in one community, they can become the "solution" they are looking for in other communities.

When we act on the proposition that people are capable of self-government, it becomes possible to experience self-government in effective operation—as effectively as any practice can live up to an ideal.

Notes

1. Jennings, "The Puny Voice of Democracy: 1.3 Percent."
2. "Across the USA."
3. The Harwood Group, research for "Meaningful Chaos."
4. Public Agenda Foundation, *Faulty Diagnosis*, 11–12.
5. Roberts, untitled report, pt. 2, 5.
6. The Harwood Group, "Meaningful Chaos," 22.
7. Personal communication with Yvonne Sims, National Issues Forums convenor, Grand Rapids, Michigan, January 1993.
8. The Harwood Group, "Meaningful Chaos," 20–29.
9. McAfee, "Interview with Ernesto Cortes, Jr.," 24.
10. Personal communication with Joan Martin-Brown, January 1993.

11. Dawkins, *The Selfish Gene*, 215.

12. "A Public Voice . . . '91." This annually produced public affairs program includes footage from National Issues Forums discussions.

13. For example, see Sanders, "Against Deliberation." Pages 4–14 lay out Sanders's case against deliberation.

14. Personal communication with James Wilder and Michael Perry, who are involved in the Youth-at-Risk Program at the Kettering Foundation, February 1993.

15. Page and Shapiro, *The Rational Public*, 390–91.

16. Geyelin, "Dean Rusk's Pursuit of Peace."

17. Page and Shapiro, *The Rational Public*, 393–95. The authors did find discrepancies between government action and citizen wishes when public attention was not focused on unpopular policies.

18. Public Agenda Foundation, *Faulty Diagnosis*, 9.

19. Yankelovich, "How Public Opinion Really Works," 102–5.

20. Page and Shapiro, *The Rational Public*, 388.

21. Outcomes of NIF deliberations can be seen in the "A Public Voice . . ." programs.

22. "A Public Voice . . . '92."

23. Johnson, *Science Policy Priorities and the Public*; Doble and Johnson, *Science and the Public*.

24. Personal communication with Robin Lambert of the Program for Rural Services and Research, University of Alabama, November 1992.

25. See Raspberry, "Cargo Cult."

26. Public Agenda Foundation, *Curbing Health Care Costs*. See 7–9, 29–31 for general information; figures cited on 15–16, 43.

27. Public Agenda Foundation, *HealthVote Network*, 5.

28. Although not always widely covered by the mainstream media, a number of such cases can be found in more specialized publications. For example, see *In Context* magazine, no. 33 (Fall 1992).

29. Booth News Service, "Kellogg Is Serious about Move"; Warner and Gruley, "If Battle Creek Voters Reject Kellogg Plan"; Warner, "Battle Creek Merger OK'd."

30. Heifetz and Sinder, "Political Leadership," 185–91.

31. Davis Merritt, Jr., December 1992, from the unpublished transcript of the Public Journalism Seminar, sponsored by the Kettering Foundation and New Directions for News, 9.

32. Ratterman, "Waste"; Allen, "Curbside Recycling Begins."

33. Spence, "A Report from Appalachia," 67.

34. The Harwood Group, "From the Heart of America," 10.

35. Brecher and Costello, *Building Bridges*, 93.

36. Focus group conducted by John Doble of John Doble Research Associates, Inc., in Bensonville, Ill., and Orange County, Calif., 1992.

37. See Barber, *Strong Democracy*.

38. This interpretation of democracy's claim owes a great deal to Hook, *The Hero in History*, 229–45, and to Sartori, *The Theory of Democracy Revisited*.

11

Reclaiming Politics

Every chapter in this book points to one conclusion: Modern America's concept of politics is too narrow. Politics is undeniably what politicians and interest groups and representative governments do. Yet, given what Americans are doing in associations and community problem solving, politics is certainly more than what the conventional wisdom says it is. As we have seen, people don't have to be enticed or forced into politics; they are already practicing politics.

What citizens feel shut out of is the formal political system. At best, the system treats them as consumers rather than responsible owners. Yet people do not have to accept that demotion, and many don't. As the *New York Times* observed in 1991, the political system itself is a political issue.[1] The solution is not to denigrate government. The solution is to create a stronger democracy—a more deliberative democracy—in order to make representative government work as it should.

To do that, citizens must take back their role in the political system. Romanticizing citizenship—idealizing citizens as virtue incarnate—won't do the job. Neither will insisting on the rights of citizens. People will take back the system when they turn their attention to responsibilities of citizenship, to the things the public must do because no one else can. We must also revive the civil institutions that link the informal political structure to the formal political system. The most basic of these are public forums and public discourse. We can't revive them, however, as long as the

conventional understanding of politics goes unexamined and un-
challenged. Citizens' unwillingness to be associated with the word
politics is testimony to the extent to which politicians and governments have appropriated to themselves a term that once belonged
to everyone. We need to understand why that has happened in order to reclaim politics.

Lessons from the Invention of Politics

Politics is a human invention. The history of politics is testimony to how much it is rooted in everyday life. Politics began
when communities no longer thought of their fate as beyond their
control but as subject to human decision making.[2] Ancient tribes
saw their lives determined by natural disasters (radical changes in
the weather, crop failures) or attacks by other tribes. They believed
that they were at the mercy of the gods' capriciousness. Slowly,
probably in fits and starts, people realized they were not simply
pawns of the fates. They began to think of controlling their own
destiny. How? By making common choices in order to improve
their chances of survival. Whether humankind prospered or per-
ished depended on the soundness of those choices. Decisions had to
be made about where to move or settle. Common decisions even
had to be made about how to make common decisions. That is,
people had to choose the rules by which they would live. The need
to make these life-or-death decisions caused people to form political communities within their social, religious, economic, and geographic communities.

Political organization was a step beyond earlier kinship or tribal
organization. The emergence of a political community that was
more than a tribal group—a community with citizens who had de-
finable roles—can be seen well before the flowering of democracy
in the fifth century B.C. The city-state, or polis, that developed in
fifth-century Greece may have had its origin in a much earlier period.[3] Perhaps democracy had its roots in the open village of the
Doric Greeks, called a demos (deme). The Doric deme was the
model for the Athenian wards (also called demes) on which classical

democracy was based. "Democracy" is usually translated to mean "rule by the people," but it can also be understood as rule by the demes. Democratic Athens was not organized as a single unit but as a city made up of subunits of wards or demes, which allowed for face-to-face deliberations. It is often said that democracy is only possible in small city-states like ancient Athens, yet even Athens was too large to function without being broken down into smaller political divisions.

It is unlikely that a democratic politics would have emerged had the civil infrastructure, the demes, and multideme districts not cut across the historic tribal cleavages of Greek society. As a result of dramatic reforms in the sixth century B.C., the old tribal system gave way to a new civil order. The new political subdivisions of Athens were deliberately constructed so that each one was a kind of political Noah's ark. People of different tribes, occupations, and regions were brought together—just as citizens.[4] Politics was invented, in a sense, to allow strangers, that is, people who were not kin, to work together.

Democracy seems to have developed in Greece as a response to the abuses that came from rule by oligarchies. The primary problem was arbitrary rule by a self-serving elite or, worse, a self-serving dictator. Remedies to this problem led to four tenets of democratic politics:

- Public deliberation is necessary to establish purpose;
- Elections are the proper means for selecting leaders (by majority determination);
- Power should be diffuse;
- Rule should be subject to law (laws reflecting the general or public interest were to serve as a further barrier to powerful leaders who might be disposed to arbitrary and self-serving actions).

Certain corollaries followed from this original formula for democracy. Active political participation was expected; it was a responsibility, not just a right. The public had both a chance to speak freely and an obligation to assemble frequently. Citizens met not only in the official assembly but also informally and beforehand in the marketplace.[5] Information about public matters had to be open to the public. These old ideas about democratic politics still inform what was earlier described as "new thinking" in the United States.

Treating Politics as a Public Matter

To reclaim a broader and richer concept of politics, it is also necessary to reclaim the meaning of *public.* The Greeks thought of politics as primarily public. There was little government. Officials served more like members of our volunteer fire departments. Although there were notable leaders like Pericles, people generally took turns holding the various offices. All citizens were expected to participate in the assemblies. Athenian juries numbered in the hundreds.[6]

The precepts of a public or citizen politics were spelled out by Pericles in the quotation introducing this part of the book. Citizen action is essential, and public deliberation is a prerequisite to political action because it instructs that action. What Pericles really said in the phrase translated as "we think of discussion as an indispensable preliminary" is that the Athenians "taught themselves first" through public deliberation before acting (*logois prodidacthania*).

People today continue to think of politics as public when they describe what they are doing to address problems that matter as a "public" activity. Understanding politics as something public helps broaden the definition of politics from things that politicians and governments do. It helps remedy the impression that politics is a separate realm with little to do with our personal lives. More than that, thinking of politics as public has practical applications. Take the case of the dilemma of some nursing-home residents who were confronted with mounting thefts. As long as the residents did not think of the thefts as public problems and did not deal with them as a public, their troubles were seen as no more than individual complaints. All that changed when residents began to think of themselves as a public and the home as a political community rather than just an institution. Problems were no longer seen and treated as individual problems; they were seen and treated as public problems. Once the residents saw themselves as a public, they were able to join forces and develop common strategies to address their problems.[7]

The difficulty today with claiming that politics is public is that the term *public* is used in very ambiguous ways. As a result, we lose some of the power in the idea of public politics. *Public* can mean the ordinary, something open to everyone, the lowest common denominator—as in public rest rooms and public transportation. The public is everyone, the mass, the many. At other times, *public* means government, as in a public official. The two words are used interchangeably. Although mayors, governors, and members of Congress are called public officials, they are really government officials. The public and the government are not the same thing. *Government* has its own distinct meaning. "To govern" originally meant to steer a ship—it meant "to control." One of the drawbacks of using the language this way is that it is more difficult to make it clear that the government is an instrument of the public for acting collectively. The government is the property of the public. *Public* and *government* are also quite different in that political relations in the public are lateral (people to people), whereas in the government they are usually vertical (from authorities to subordinates). When we confuse the terms, we tend to assume that all relations in politics are hierarchical.

The public realm is older, more inclusive, and more fundamental than the world of government. The public is pregovernmental in that the work of the public in setting directions precedes steering or controlling. In his book on the public, Parker Palmer argues that the public is around us all the time.[8] We experience it every day. Yet like air, which is also around us all of the time, we may not be very aware of what is public. Not being aware of the public contributes to the tendency to think that all politics has to do with is government. We lose sight of politics as basically a public activity.

John Dewey said that "the outstanding problem of the Public is the discovery and identification of itself."[9] A public that is invisible robs us of a sense of what it offers us. From Palmer's point of view, when we lack an awareness of the public, we fail to appreciate the opportunity it offers. "So public life, which could be a force for unity, and a stimulating dimension of individual experience, lies fallow."[10]

Teenagers in Harry Boyte's public life project confirmed the validity of this observation. They found the term a useful descriptor for that part of their lives that was not private and social. College students in the Harwood interviews, on the other hand, complained about the lack of a public language needed to talk about what was political in their lives and not governmental or partisan.[11]

A richer concept of the public is suggested in the word's origin. The term seems to have roots in some combination of the Latin word for people, *populus*, with the term for maturity, *pubes*. Those who used the word *public* to refer to a body of mature adults, presumably people who had that sense of responsibility we associate with adults, help us see a distinction between a public and a crowd of people. A public isn't just a group of people, not even the inhabitants of a particular city or state. In its richest sense, a public consists of people with a certain relationship to one another—the kind of relationship that occurs among responsible adults. In this sort of relationship, people are obliged (as adults) to understand their connections to one another and the consequences of those connections. Simply put, a public can be thought of as a group of diverse but responsible human beings—a society of citizens.

In families, relationships are determined by kinship: father or daughter, aunt or uncle. In politics and public life, on the other hand, we have to deal with people who are not kin but are strangers. So "family" would be the wrong metaphor for a public. We have to deal with strangers because we want to accomplish things we cannot do alone. As a result, we often have to turn to these "others" who share our space, our neighborhood, our community, our country. These strangers, whom we need in order to reach common objectives, become important to us. We don't have to love or like them; we do have to work with them. So we invest in a range of public relationships, not out of sentiment, but out of a political necessity. And when this happens, we are no longer a mass but a company of strangers.[12]

People become a public when they acknowledge their interconnectedness and the consequences of their ties with others—over extended time. To be fully public is to be cognizant of our connectedness. It is to be as aware as we can be of the consequences of our

actions on the whole of the places where we live. This understanding of the public forces us to deal simultaneously with both past and
future. A sense of the past heightens a people's awareness of their
interdependence; the prospect of the future heightens their appreciation for consequences.

To think of politics as a public activity changes the very meaning
of politics. Politics becomes the art of making productive relationships among diverse people, rather than just passing legislation or
electing representatives.

Public versus Private?

Politics in America also has to do with what is private. Our
laws protect the right of privacy, private property, and private con-
science. We lead private lives and value our privacy. We associate
privacy with freedom, believing the total loss of privacy to be the
total loss of freedom. However, it is a mistake to treat privacy and
publicness as if they were opposites or to attempt to find just the
right balance between the two. The history of our country is filled
with debates over whether we have placed too much emphasis on
individuals and their privacy and too little on the common good.
Although those debates may have their uses, the "perfect balance"
they try to identify will always elude us.

Framing the debate as one of individual privacy versus public
good is artificial. It suggests that there is such a thing as a purely
private individual who exists like some isolated planet in space.
There is no such person. The framing also suggests there is a public
that can exist apart from the well-being of the individuals in it.
There is no such public. That would be some kind of collectivity
where people have no being except for their existence as a part of
the collective order.

What is private and what is public are not antithetical; they are two
sides of the same coin. They have an innate relationship. It is impossible to think of an individual apart from a social context (unless we
mean hermits). And it is impossible to think of any public order apart
from diverse and free human beings (unless we mean a sect).

The close connection between what is public and what is private is suggested by the history of the concept of personal freedom. Words for individual freedom have their roots in words that mean to belong to, or be part of, a group—a polity. To be free personally meant to belong—to be a part of a nation, to be a citizen, not a slave. Of course, that doesn't mean humans can be thought of as cogs in a collective order. But neither can they be understood as totally independent, go-it-alone atoms. We exist as individuals in relation to one another—that is what it means to be human.[13]

The point is that what is personal and private and what is public and shared are actually complementary. If we tried to be totally individualistic and private, individuality and diversity themselves would be in jeopardy. Parker Palmer goes so far as to say, "The very health of the private realm depends on the health of the public sphere." The public realm is the human environment in which the private exists. If people do not care about common life, then there is no way that private life can provide security for individuals. There are too many threats to that security from common life gone bad, from runaway pollution or runaway crime. If the public environment is unhealthy, then private life will inevitably suffer.[14]

The challenge is to understand the relationship between what is public and what is private. A professor of policy studies at the University of Alabama, Robert McKenzie, has a simple exercise for helping students appreciate that relationship. First, he asks students to list their individual goals on a card. Next, he asks them to take another card and list the characteristics of the world in which they want to live. The first card usually has goals that point inward, for example, a desire for greater self-understanding. The second usually ranks social justice and world peace as public objectives. McKenzie then asks the obvious question: How does the class propose to get from the goals on the first card to the objectives listed on the second?[15]

Acting as Though We Belong

Because public life is shared life in all its forms, people don't have to go out, forget their personal concerns, and be unselfish in order to be responsible members of a public. Passing along a sense of duty and civic responsibility protects a society from a culture of selfishness. Yet the people who work in community associations didn't leave their personal interests at home when they joined with others to solve common problems. The people in the Harwood interviews who described their public activities didn't think they were being particularly unselfish. Good politics is compatible with normal behavior. Sainthood is not a prerequisite.

Being public and being political are simply behaving as though we belong. Behaving as though we belong is the way we act in our church or synagogue or at a reunion. We feel at home and act accordingly. We are aware of how our behaviors affect others, the place we are in, and the relationships we want to maintain. No one has to tell us that. Yet, we take responsibility for the consequences of our actions in ways that we don't take in places where we don't think we belong.

Similarly, we belong in the public affairs of our time; we belong in our community and in our country. Acting as though we belong begins in claiming responsibility for the way we act. Recall Bertha Gilkey and her neighbors in Cochran Gardens. They acted as though they belonged; they claimed their responsibilities as citizens of the housing project.

Other words for political participation reinforce the idea that belonging or being part of the whole is at the heart of what it means to participate. Our political vocabulary is full of words that mean to associate, to share, to communicate, or to have in common. They do not suggest that we lose our personal identity. We can be part of the whole of our country or community without compromising our uniqueness. Think of the relation of the different keys on a piano. They belong together. They are different but have much in common. Lose any one and the keyboard is ruined.[16]

This fuller sense of participation takes us beyond the conventional notion that participation is just the exercise of a legal right. In a democracy, it is not the majority that rules—it is only the majority of those who participate that rules. Saying that participation is a legal right doesn't help us very much without an understanding of how we are to act when we participate. Merely going about asserting our rights to one another would make for a rather contentious and empty polity. And to whom would we go to claim our rights? Do we have to be empowered by someone else? The notion of participation as acting as though we belong means that we can act on our own authority. We do not have to be empowered by anyone else. The participants in the Naugatuck Valley project and the clean water project on the Tennessee River did what they did on their own authority.

Not in the Majority but Still in the Public

The idea that we belong in politics and public life is also a healthy antidote to some implications of majoritarian politics. If we lose in the elections, if we are in the minority, we feel that we are on the outside looking in. Certainly, if our party loses an election, we are outside the government. Someone else takes our seats in the legislature and the executive offices. But we are never outside the public. We always belong there.

A public is more than an electorate. An electorate is an aggregation of people who vote to make decisions. A public is an integrated body. And a public does more than vote. We only vote on those matters we cannot resolve any other way. There are other, more integrative ways of coming together to decide and act. They were described by people active in community-based organizations, like those in the Lake Union project, who worked to develop a consensus rather than just create a majority.

The Politics That Goes beyond Solving Problems

Politics is certainly about solving common problems, but it is more. Although politics is practical, it is not purely instrumental. Politics is a creative activity in that it has to do with building the kind of community and country we want for ourselves and our children. In fact, it has to do with creating the kind of people we want to be. To repeat, politics is about transformation, not just transactions. In ancient Greece, the political community—the polis—was not just a city, a place to live to pursue private ends. The polis was a political community joined together to realize the good life in common and the fullest potential of human beings.

Richard King, who writes on American civil rights, captures this transformative power of politics in his stories of the citizens who became active in "the movement."[17] King suggests that the uniqueness of the movement was in its creation of a new sense of self through political participation. The experiences of the movement, particularly the public meetings, gave the participants a new way to talk among themselves and, from that, a new way to think about themselves. It was a powerful experience. People who had never thought of themselves as citizens came to think of themselves very much as citizens. And they would go to any lengths—even to the point of risking their lives—to defend their citizenship. The experience was both frightening and exhilarating. King quotes Unita Blackwell, who later became the mayor of Mayersville, Mississippi: "We found ourselves involved in working in political work, and although we haven't figured everything out," she said, "it's been just wonderful."[18]

Engaging in politics expands people's sense of themselves. Adding a political dimension to someone's life doesn't take away from his or her individuality by pressing that person into a collective mold. As Benjamin Barber explains, what happens in politics is somewhat like what happens when people marry. Married people do not cease to have a personal identity; rather, their identity takes on new meaning because of the marriage. If children are born, the parents don't say, "Darn, now we have to divide what we have three ways." The child adds to parents' evolving sense of themselves. The child is not a third party but an expression of who they have become—parents.[19] In the same sense, public responsibilities can actually change our identity as the scope of what we are willing to take responsibility for changes.

While the purpose of politics is not personal therapy, the concept of personal growth through public participation is consistent with the earliest concepts of politics. The Athenians believed that engagement in public affairs kept people from becoming "idiots," or purely private beings. (For the Greeks, an idiot was not someone with a low IQ but someone who knew nothing of his or her connection to the world outside the purely personal.) Participating in public life transforms people from private individuals into public citizens. Although not the goal of participation, it is a serendipitous benefit.

The revolutionary power of politics is not in creating advocates for particular policies but in actually transforming people so they no longer see themselves as victims of the system, waiting to be empowered by someone else, or as critical consumers of the available political solutions, or—heaven forbid—as exploiters who have learned all too well the skills of influencing others. The highest use of politics is to create true citizens, people aware of and active in the exercise of their inherent capacities as they go about the business of creating better communities and better countries.[20] Politics is self-recreating. Political freedom becomes not just "freedom from" but "freedom to."[21]

When Americans act together in their communities to expand the common ground and solve problems, when they create associations, when they organize forums, they are making politics their own. And they are redefining politics by the way they practice it. They are reclaiming the earlier and richer meanings of politics. In that expanded notion of politics, the public and its citizens are not peripheral, they are central.

Notes

1. "The Missing Campaign, Pinch-Hitting for the Democrats."

2. Meier, *The Greek Discovery of Politics*, 1–5, 22–25.

3. Ehrenberg, *The Greek State*, 39–52. For additional information, see Forrest, *The Emergence of Greek Democracy*.

4. Hansen, *The Athenian Democracy in the Age of Demosthenes*, 46–49; Forrest, *The Emergence of Greek Democracy*.

5. Barber and Watson, *The Struggle for Democracy*, 2.

6. Ehrenberg, *The Greek State*, 52–53, 65–66, 73.

7. The Hubert H. Humphrey Institute of Public Affairs, *Public Life*, 1–2.

8. See Palmer, *The Company of Strangers*.

9. Dewey, *The Public and Its Problems*, 185.

10. Palmer, *The Company of Strangers*, 34.

11. The Harwood Group, *College Students Talk Politics*, vii.

12. Palmer, *The Company of Strangers*, 17–33.

13. Gould, *Rethinking Democracy*, 74–75.

14. Palmer, *The Company of Strangers*, 31.

15. McKenzie, "Teaching Public Leadership," 12–13.

16. Follett, *The New State*, 336–37.

17. See King, "Citizenship and Self-Respect."

18. Ibid., 22.

19. London, "The Politics of Education and the Future of America," 6–7.

20. See Pitkin and Shumer, "On Participation."

21. Gould, *Rethinking Democracy*, 84–85.

Bibliography

"Across the USA: News from Every State." *USA Today*, August 26, 1992, 7A.

Allen, Barbara. "Curbside Recycling Begins." *Oxford Press*, February 13, 1992, 1.

Andrain, Charles F. *Children and Civic Awareness: A Study in Political Education*. Columbus: Charles E. Merrill Publishing Company, 1971.

Arendt, Hannah. *On Revolution*. New York: Penguin Books, 1963.

Barber, Benjamin R. "The Civic Mission of the University." *Kettering Review* (Fall 1989): 62–72.

———. *Strong Democracy: Participatory Politics for a New Age*. Berkeley: University of California Press, 1984.

Barber, Benjamin R., and Patrick Watson. *The Struggle for Democracy*. Boston: Little, Brown and Company, 1988.

Bell, Jeffrey. *Populism and Elitism: Politics in the Age of Equality*. Washington, D.C.: Regnery Gateway, 1992.

Benedetto, Richard. "For Most, Political System Is Working." *USA Today*, January 17, 1992, 2A.

———. "Voter Unease Over-rated, 61 Percent Back Incumbents." *USA Today*, January 17, 1992, 1A.

Bluestone, Barry, and Bennett Harrison. *The Deindustrialization of America*. New York: Basic Books, Inc., 1982.

Bolling, Richard. "Statement Before the Committee on Governmental Affairs of the U.S. Senate (May 20, 1981)." *Index of Congressional Committee Hearings*. Washington: Government Printing Office, 1963–84.

Booth News Service. "Kellogg Is Serious about Move." *Kalamazoo Gazette*, October 12, 1982, 14A.

Boyte, Harry. *Commonwealth: A Return to Citizen Politics.* New York: Free Press, 1989.

———. *Community Is Possible: Repairing America's Roots.* New York: Harper and Row, 1984.

———. "The Growth of Citizen Politics: Stages in Local Community Organizing." *Dissent* 37 (Fall 1990): 513–18.

Brecher, Jeremy, and Tim Costello, eds. *Building Bridges: The Emerging Grassroots Coalition of Labor and Community.* New York: Monthly Review Press, 1990.

Breuer, Rebecca, ed. *Teaching Politics: The 1991 Project Public Life Annual Report.* Minneapolis: Humphrey Center, University of Minnesota, 1991.

Brown, Richard D. *Revolutionary Politics in Massachusetts: The Boston Committee of Correspondence and the Towns, 1772–1774.* Cambridge: Harvard University Press, 1970.

Brown, Robert E. *Middle-Class Democracy and the Revolution in Massachusetts, 1691–1780.* Ithaca: Cornell University Press, 1955.

Bryan, Frank, and John McClaughry. *The Vermont Papers: Recreating Democracy on a Human Scale.* Chelsea: Chelsea Green Publishing Co., 1989.

Bryce, James. *The American Commonwealth.* New York: Macmillan and Co., 1891.

Campaign for Human Development. "Naugatuck Valley Residents Assert the Primacy of Community." *Campaign for Human Development: Annual Report, Anniversary Edition.* 1985–86. Available from the Campaign for Human Development, Washington, D.C.

Campbell, Colin. "Clinton's Little Tic." *Atlanta Constitution,* February 14, 1993, 1F.

Cheney, Richard. "A Difference of Perception." *Kettering Review* (Summer 1983): 17–18.

Chrislip, David, and Andrea Williams. *A Sense of Community: An Essential Part of Creating Community Change through Collaborative Leadership.* Minneapolis: National Civic League Press, 1991.

Cohen, Sharon. "Tenants Bring Pride, Efficiency as Managers of Housing Projects." *Los Angeles Times,* March 24, 1991, A12.

Conover, Pamela J., Ivor M. Crewe, and Donald M. Searing. "The Nature of Citizenship in the United States and Great Britain: Empirical Comments on Theoretical Themes." *Journal of Politics* 53 (August 1991): 800–832.

Cooper, Terry L. "Citizenship and Professionalism in Public Administration." *Public Administration Review* 44 (March 1984): 143–49.

Cousins, Norman. *Human Options.* New York: W. W. Norton and Company, 1981.

Dahl, Robert A. *Democracy and Its Critics.* New Haven: Yale University Press, 1961.

Daniels, Bruce C. *The Connecticut Town: Growth and Development, 1635–1790.* Middletown: Wesleyan University Press, 1979.

Dawkins, Richard. *The Selfish Gene.* Oxford: Oxford University Press, 1976.

Dewey, John. *The Public and Its Problems.* Athens: Ohio University Press, 1954.

Diggins, John Patrick. "From Pragmatism to Natural Law: Walter Lippmann's Quest for the Foundation of Legitimacy." *Political Theory* 19 (November 1991): 519–38.

Dionne, E. J., Jr. *Why Americans Hate Politics.* New York: Simon and Schuster, 1991.

Doble, John. "An Analysis of Results from Two Focus Groups for Use in the Production of 'A Public Voice' Video on People and Politics." Mimeographed. New York: John Doble Research Associates, Inc., November 9, 1992.

Doble, John, and Jean Johnson. *Science and the Public: A Report in Three Volumes.* New York: Public Agenda Foundation, 1990.

Dorchester Antiquarian and Historical Society. *History of the Town of Dorchester, Massachusetts.* Boston: E. Clapp, Jr., 1859.

Dye, Thomas R., and L. Harmon Zeigler. *The Irony of Democracy: An Uncommon Introduction to American Politics.* North Scituate: Duxbury Press, 1978.

Edwards, Newton, and Herman G. Richey. *The School in the American Social Order.* Boston: Houghton Mifflin Company, 1963.

Ehrenberg, Victor. *The Greek State.* New York: W. W. Norton and Company, Inc., 1960.

Ehrenhalt, Alan. *The United States of Ambition: Politicians, Power, and the Pursuit of Office.* New York: Times Books, 1991.

Elazar, Daniel J. "America and the Federalist Revolution." *This World,* no. 10 (1985): 52–71.

———. "Harmonizing Government Organization with the Political Tradition." *Publius* 8 (1978): 49–58.

Elazar, Daniel J., and John Kincaid. "Covenant and Polity." *New Conversations* 4 (1979): 4–8.

Elshtain, Jean Bethke. "Democracy and the QUBE Tube." *Nation*, August 7–14, 1982, 108.

Erickson, Bonnie H., and T. A. Nosanchuk. "How a Political Association Politicizes." *Canadian Review of Sociology and Anthropology* 27 (May 1990): 206–19.

Etzioni, Amitai. *The Moral Dimension: Toward a New Economics.* New York: Free Press, 1988.

Evans, Sara M., and Harry C. Boyte. *Free Spaces: The Sources of Democratic Change in America.* New York: Harper and Row, 1986.

Fishkin, James S. *Democracy and Deliberation: New Directions for Democratic Reform.* New Haven: Yale University Press, 1991.

Follett, Mary Parker. *The New State: Group Organization: The Solution of Popular Government.* 1920. Reprint. Gloucester: Peter Smith, 1965.

Foreman, Dave. *Confessions of an Eco-Warrior.* New York: Harmony Books, 1991.

Forrest, William G. G. *The Emergence of Greek Democracy: The Character of Greek Politics, 800–400 B.C.* London: Weidenfeld and Nicolson, 1966.

Frank, Glenn. "The Parliament of the People." *The Century Magazine* 98 (1919): 401–16.

Fry-Winchester, Kay. "New Solution to an Old Problem." *Vermont Catholic Tribune.*

Gardner, John W. "Building Community." *Kettering Review* (Fall 1989): 73–81.

———. *Toward a Pluralistic but Coherent Society.* New York: Aspen Institute for Humanistic Studies, 1980.

Geyelin, Philip. "Dean Rusk's Pursuit of Peace." *Washington Post*, February 8, 1984, A19.

Giamatti, A. Bartlett. *The University and the Public Interest.* New York: Atheneum, 1981.

Gould, Carol C. *Rethinking Democracy.* Cambridge: Cambridge University Press, 1988.

Graham, Pauline. *Dynamic Managing: The Follett Way.* London: Professional Publishing Limited, 1987.

Gurwitt, Rob. "The Rule of the Absentocracy: The Eclipse of Hometown Leadership and How Some Places Are Coping with It." *Governing* 4 (September 1991): 52–58.

Hale, Dennis, Marc Landy, and Wilson C. McWilliams. "Freedom, Civic Virtue, and the Failure of Our Constitution." *Freedom at Issue* 89 (May–June 1985): 12–15.

Hallett, Stanley J. "Communities Can Plan Future on Their Own Terms." *Regeneration* 6 (January–February 1990): 8–9.

Hansen, Mogens Herman. *The Athenian Democracy in the Age of Demosthenes: Structure, Principles and Ideology.* Translated by J. A. Crook. Cambridge: Basil Blackwell, Ltd., 1991.

Harwood, Richard C. *The Public's Role in the Policy Process: A View from State and Local Policymakers.* Dayton: Kettering Foundation, 1989.

The Harwood Group. *Citizens and Politics: A View from Main Street America.* Dayton: Kettering Foundation, 1991.

———. *College Students Talk Politics.* Dayton: Kettering Foundation, 1993.

———. "From the Heart of America: Whither the American Consensus? A Summary of Seven Focus Groups Conducted for Knight-Ridder." Unpublished report, August 1992.

———. "Meaningful Chaos: How People Form Relationships with Public Concerns." Unpublished report, December 31, 1992.

———. "The Public-Government Disconnection Project: Project Objectives." Unpublished report, May 6, 1992.

———. "The Public-Government Disconnection Project: St. Joseph Action Research Field Notes." Unpublished reports, September 4, 1992, October 28–29, 1992.

Havel, Vaclav. "The End of the Modern Era." *New York Times,* March 1, 1992, E15.

Heifetz, Ronald, and Riley Sinder. "Political Leadership: Managing the Public's Problem Solving." In *The Power of Public Ideas.* Edited by Robert B. Reich. Cambridge: Ballinger Publishing Company, 1988.

Hobbes, Thomas. *Leviathan.* Parts 1 and 2. Indianapolis: Bobbs-Merrill Educational Publishing, 1958.

Holton, Gerald. "Where Is Science Taking Us?" Paper presented at the Jefferson Symposium, Washington, D.C., and Boston, May 11–13, 1981.

Hook, Sidney. *The Hero in History.* 1943. Reprint. Atlantic Highlands: Humanities Press International, Inc., 1966.

The Hubert H. Humphrey Institute of Public Affairs. *Public Life: The Newsletter of Project Public Life* 3 (March–April 1991): 1–11.

Jefferson, Thomas. *Writings.* Notes by Merrill D. Peterson. New York: Library of America, 1984.

Jennings, Max. "The Puny Voice of Democracy: 1.3 Percent." *Dayton Daily News*, August 9, 1992, 8B.

Johnson, Jean. *Science Policy Priorities and the Public.* New York: Public Agenda Foundation, 1989.

Katz, Jeffrey L. "Neighborhood Politics: A Changing World." *Governing* 4 (November 1990): 48–54.

Ketcham, Ralph. *The Anti-Federalist Papers and the Constitutional Convention Debates.* New York: New American Library, 1986.

———. *Individualism and Public Life.* New York: Basil Blackwell, Ltd., 1987.

King, Richard H. "Citizenship and Self-Respect: The Experience of Politics in the Civil Rights Movement." *Journal of American Studies* 22 (1988): 7–24.

Knoll, Erwin. "Making My Vote Count by Refusing to Cast It." *Peace and Democracy News* 5 (Summer 1991): 19–20, 49.

Kuhns, Maude Pinney. *The "Mary and John": A Story of the Founding of Dorchester, Massachusetts, 1630.* Rutland: Tuttle Publishing Co., 1943.

Landers, Robert K. "Why America Doesn't Vote." *Editorial Research Reports*, February 19, 1988, 82–94.

Lasswell, Harold D. *Politics: Who Gets What, When, How.* Magnolia: Peter Smith Publishers, 1958.

Laumann, Edward O., and David Knoke. *The Organizational State: Social Choice in National Policy Domains.* Madison: University of Wisconsin Press, 1987.

Leo, John. "Community and Personal Duty." *U.S. News & World Report*, January 28, 1991, 17.

London, Scott. "'The Politics of Education and the Future of America': An Interview with Benjamin Barber." *Afternoon Insights* on WYSO-FM, Yellow Springs, Ohio, December 14, 1992.

Lowi, Theodore J. *The End of Liberalism: The Second Republic of the United States.* New York: W. W. Norton and Company, 1979.

Maass, Arthur. *Congress and the Common Good.* New York: Basic Books, 1983.

Main, Jackson Turner. *The Antifederalists: Critics of the Constitution, 1781–1788.* Chicago: University of Chicago Press, 1961.

Mansbridge, Jane. *Beyond Adversary Democracy.* New York: Basic Books, 1980.

Mathews, David, and Noëlle McAfee. *Community Politics.* 2d rev. ed. Dayton: Kettering Foundation, 1992.

Mathews, David, Noëlle McAfee, and Robert McKenzie. *Hard Choices.* Dayton: Kettering Foundation, 1990.

McAfee, Noëlle. "Interview with Ernesto Cortes, Jr.: On Leadership." Unpublished manuscript, November 19, 22, 1992. Published excerpt as "Relationship and Power." *Kettering Review* (Summer 1993).

McGregor, Eugene B. "The Great Paradox of Democratic Citizenship and Public Personnel Administration." *Public Administration Review* 44 (March 1984): 126.

McKenzie, Robert H. "Teaching Public Leadership." Mimeographed. Tuscaloosa: University of Alabama, 1987.

McKnight, John. "Do No Harm: Policy Options That Meet Human Needs." *Social Policy* 20 (Summer 1989): 5–15.

———. "Regenerating Community." *Kettering Review* (Fall 1989): 40–50.

McKnight, John, and John Kretzmann. "Community Organizing in the 1980s: Toward a Post-Alinsky Agenda." *Social Policy* 14 (Winter 1984): 15–17.

Meier, Christian. *The Greek Discovery of Politics.* Translated by David McLintock. Cambridge: Harvard University Press, 1990.

Melville, Keith. *The Domestic Policy Association: A Report on Its First Year.* Dayton: Kettering Foundation, 1983.

———. "Introducing the National Issues Forum." In *On Second Thought: Citizens and Leaders Address Three of the Nation's Pressing Issues.* Edited by Keith Melville. Dayton: Kettering Foundation, 1984.

"The Missing Campaign: Pinch-Hitting for the Democrats." *New York Times*, July 21, 1991, 18A.

Moore, Carl M. *A Working Paper on Community.* Fairfax: National Conference on Peacemaking and Conflict Resolution, 1991.

Myczack, Leaf. "We're the Solution." *In Context* 28 (Spring 1991): 16–19.

Nagourney, Adam. "Clinton Faces 'Challenges We Wanted.'" *USA Today*, November 5, 1992, 1A.

National Association of Community Leadership Organizations. *Exploring Leadership.* Alexandria: National Association of Community Leadership, 1984.

National Commission on Neighborhoods, Task Force on Governance, Citizen Participation and Neighborhood Empowerment. *People Building Neighborhoods: Case Study Appendix.* Volume 1. Washington: National Commission on Neighborhoods, 1979.

Novak, Michael. "Mediating Institutions: The Communitarian Individual in America." *Public Interest* 68 (1982): 3–20.

Oliver, Leonard P. *The Art of Citizenship: Public Issue Forums*. Dayton: Kettering Foundation, 1983.

Oreskes, Michael. "Alienation from Government Grows, Poll Finds." *New York Times*, September 19, 1990, A26.

Orren, Gary R. "Beyond Self-Interest." In *The Power of Public Ideas*. Edited by Robert B. Reich. Cambridge: Ballinger Publishing Company, 1988.

Osborne, David, and Ted Gaebler. *Reinventing Government: How the Entrepreneurial Spirit Is Transforming the Public Sector*. Reading: Addison-Wesley Publishers, 1992.

Overstreet, Harry A., and Bonaro W. Overstreet. *Town Meeting Comes to Town*. New York: Harper and Brothers Publishers, 1938.

Page, Benjamin I., and Robert Y. Shapiro. *The Rational Public: Fifty Years of Trends in Americans' Policy Preferences*. Chicago: University of Chicago Press, 1992.

Palmer, Parker. *The Company of Strangers: Christians and the Renewal of America's Public Life*. New York: Crossroad Publishing, 1985.

Pear, Robert. "55 Percent Voting Rate Reverses 30-Year Decline." *New York Times*, November 5, 1992, B4.

Perry, Michael J. *Citizens and Policymakers in Community Forums: Observations from the National Issues Forums*. Dayton: Kettering Foundation, 1990.

Pitkin, Hanna F., and Sara M. Shumer. "On Participation." *Democracy* 2 (1982): 43–54.

Pole, J. R. *The American Constitution For and Against: The Federalist and Anti-Federalist Papers*. New York: Hill and Wang, 1987.

Prewitt, Kenneth. "Scientific Illiteracy and Democratic Theory." *Daedalus* 112 (1983): 49–64.

Price, Tom. "Poll Says Campaign Pleased Voters." *Dayton Daily News*, November 15, 1992, 1A, 13A.

Price, Tom, and Adrianne Flynn. "Alternative Democracy." Three-part series. *Dayton Daily News*, February 2–4, 1992.

Program for Community Problem Solving. *Community Problem Solving Case Summaries*. Volume 2. Washington: Program for Community Problem Solving, 1989.

Public Agenda Foundation. *Curbing Health Care Costs: The Public's Prescription*. New York: Public Agenda Foundation, 1983.

———. *Faulty Diagnosis: Public Misconceptions about Health Care Reform*. New York: Public Agenda Foundation, 1992.

————. *HealthVote Network: Your Chance to Help Your Community Choose.* New York: Public Agenda Foundation, 1983.

————. *The Public, the Soviets, and Nuclear Arms: A Perspective from Community Leaders.* New York: Public Agenda Foundation, 1986.

"A Public Voice . . . '91." Public affairs program. New York: Milton B. Hoffman Productions, 1991. Available from the Kettering Foundation, Dayton, Ohio.

"A Public Voice . . . '92." Public affairs program. New York: Milton B. Hoffman Productions, 1992. Available from the Kettering Foundation, Dayton, Ohio.

Quigley, Charles N., ed. *Civitas: A Framework for Civic Education.* Calabasas: Center for Civic Education, 1991.

Raspberry, William. "Cargo Cult." *Washington Post,* January 3, 1985, A19.

————. "Citizens' Juries." *Washington Post,* January 23, 1993, 19A.

Ratterman, Bob. "Waste, Recycling Bids Both Likely to Be Rumpke's." *Oxford Press,* November 14, 1991, 1.

Renshon, Stanley Allen. *Psychological Needs and Political Behavior: A Theory of Personality and Political Efficacy.* New York: Free Press, 1974.

Reppetto, Thomas A. "About Crime: With Order Comes Safety." *Newsday,* June 5, 1990, 58.

Richardson, Elliot. "We Delegated Our Powers." Paper presented at the Fourth Presidential Library Conference, Ann Arbor, Michigan, March 18, 1986.

Roberts, Rona. Untitled report. November 14, 1993 [1992]. Available from the Kettering Foundation, Dayton, Ohio.

Rossiter, Clinton, and James Lare, eds. *The Essential Lippmann: A Political Philosophy for Liberal Democracy.* Cambridge: Harvard University Press, 1963.

Sandel, Michael J. "Democrats and Community: A Public Philosophy for American Liberalism." *New Republic,* February 22, 1988.

Sanders, Lynn M. "Against Deliberation." Paper presented at the Midwest Political Science Association, Chicago, Illinois, April 18–20, 1991.

Santiago Nino, Carlos. *Deliberative Democracy and the Complexity of Constitutionalism.* New York: Columbia University Press, in press.

Sartori, Giovanni. *The Theory of Democracy Revisited.* 2 vols. Chatham: Chatham House Publishers, Inc., 1987.

Saunders, Harold, and Gennady Chufrin. "A Public Peace Process." *Negotiation Journal* 9 (April 1993): 155–77.

Schneider, William. "A Loud Vote for Change." *National Journal*, November 7, 1992, 2,542–44.

Schumpeter, Joseph A. *Capitalism, Socialism and Democracy.* New York: Harper Torchbooks, 1976.

Smith, Adam. *An Inquiry into the Nature and Causes of the Wealth of Nations.* New York: Modern Library, 1937.

Spence, Beth. "A Report from Appalachia." *Future Choices* 3, no. 1 (1991): 65–70.

Spragens, Thomas A. *Reason and Democracy.* Durham: Duke University Press, 1990.

Stark, James H. *Dorchester Day: Celebration of the Two Hundred and Seventy-ninth Anniversary of the Settlement of Dorchester.* Boston: City Printing Department, 1909.

Stone, Walter J. *Republic at Risk: Self-Interest in American Politics.* Pacific Grove: Brooks-Cole Publishing Co., 1990.

Stone, William F. *The Psychology of Politics.* New York: Free Press, 1974.

Stuck, Dorothy D. "The Wilowe Institute." Brochure. Little Rock: Wilowe Institute, 1982.

Susskind, Lawrence E. "Resolving Environmental Disputes Through Ad Hocracy." *Environmental Consensus* 4 (Summer 1980): 3–5.

Taylor, Robert J., ed. *Massachusetts, Colony to Commonwealth: Documents on the Formation of Its Constitution, 1775–1780.* Chapel Hill: University of North Carolina Press, 1961.

Tocqueville, Alexis de. *Democracy in America.* Edited by J. P. Mayer. Translated by George Lawrence. Garden City: Doubleday and Company, 1969.

Uhlaner, Carole Jean. "Electoral Participation: Summing up a Decade." *Society* 28 (July–August 1991): 35–40.

Verba, Sidney, and Norman H. Nie. *Participation in America: Politics, Democracy and Social Equality.* New York: Harper and Row, 1972.

Vineyard Project. *The Vineyard* [Dayton] (Spring 1990): 1–3.

Vogler, David J., and Sidney R. Waldman. *Congress and Democracy.* Washington: Congressional Quarterly Press, 1985.

"The Voters, Yes. But Which Ones?" *New York Times*, April 10, 1992, 36A.

Warden, Gerard Byrce. "Boston Politics, 1692–1765." Ph.D dissertation, Yale University, 1966.

Warner, Robert. "Battle Creek Merger OK'd." *Kalamazoo Gazette*, November 3, 1982, 1A.

Warner, Robert, and Bryan Gruley. "If Battle Creek Voters Reject Kellogg Plan, It's Snap, Crackle, Goodbye." *Kalamazoo Gazette*, October 31, 1982, 1G.

Webster, Daniel. *The Works of Daniel Webster.* Volume 1. Boston: Little, Brown and Company, 1853.

Weil, Simone. *Oppression and Liberty.* Amherst: University of Massachusetts Press, 1973.

Wilder, James, and Michael Perry. "Hard Talk Discussion Group Report: Insights into How Citizens Talk about Education and Community." Mimeographed. Dayton: Kettering Foundation, July–August 1991.

Will, George F. *Statecraft as Soulcraft: What Government Does.* New York: Simon and Schuster, 1983.

Yankelovich, Daniel. *Coming to Public Judgment: Making Democracy Work in a Complex World.* Syracuse: Syracuse University Press, 1991.

———. "How Public Opinion Really Works." *Fortune*, October 5, 1992, 102–5.

———. *New Rules: Searching for Self-Fulfillment in a World Turned Upside Down.* New York: Random House, 1981.

Zuckerman, Michael. *Peaceable Kingdoms: New England Towns in the Eighteenth Century.* New York: Alfred A. Knopf, 1970.

Index

DAVID MATHEWS, who is president of the Kettering Foundation, was secretary of health, education, and welfare in the Ford administration and, before that, president of the University of Alabama. He received a Ph.D. in philosophy from Columbia University and taught American political and social history for nearly twenty years. As chair of the Council on Public Policy Education and one of the organizers of the National Issues Forums, he has worked to revive the tradition of the American town meeting and the practice of deliberative democracy. He has written on the relationship between the public and foundations, higher education, and government, as well as on the public's role in community development and educational reform.